OCR
GCSE POETRY ANTHOLOGY
Student Book

Annie Fox

Angela Topping

Carmel Waldron

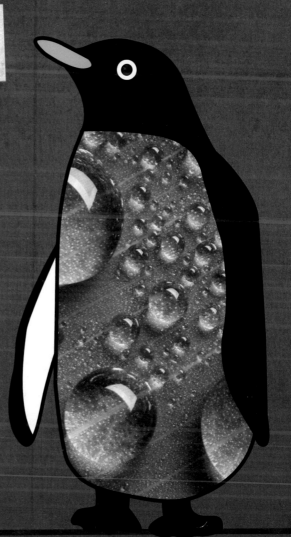

OCR
RECOGNISING ACHIEVEMENT
Official Publisher Partnership

OXFORD
UNIVERSITY PRESS

OxBox

Contents

Section 3: Contemporary Poets

Section 1
Poetry Skills

HOW TO USE THIS BOOK

The aim of this book is to help you use your OCR Poetry Anthology – *Reflections* – for your GCSE English Literature examination in contemporary poetry, and your Controlled Assessment in literary heritage poetry. It has been written in consultation with OCR by several practising teachers and Teachit contributors. It contains fun activities to help you build up your skills and knowledge about the imagery, language and structure of the poetry you are studying, so that you can write effectively about your personal response to a poem. It also gives you all the help and advice you need to tackle your assessments.

Throughout this book you will find page references for the Anthology, so that you can quickly find the poems that are being discussed. This book includes a range of helpful **features**, including the following.

- **Learning checklists** at the start of each section offer invaluable guidance on preparing for exams and Controlled Assessments to help you achieve your best results.
- **How to approach** sections outline the requirements of each part of the specification.
- **Stretch your skills** boxes offer fun activities to help you take your skills further and to find out more about a poet or poem.
- **Exam-style questions** and sample Controlled Assessment tasks, modelled on real papers, help you to practise and feel more confident.

- **Sample student responses** show examples of answers with detailed examiner's comments to help you develop and improve your own work.

You will use the *Reflections* Anthology in two units of the OCR GCSE English Literature specification:

- Unit 1: Literary Heritage Linked Texts
- Unit 4: Literary Heritage Prose and Contemporary Poetry

Each of these units is assessed using different Assessment Objectives, and the chapters in this book help you to learn what is expected from you for each objective.

The relevant Assessment Objectives (AOs) for English Literature are:

AO1 (for contemporary poetry)
Respond to texts critically and imaginatively; select and evaluate relevant textual detail to illustrate and support interpretations.

AO2 (for contemporary poetry)
Explain how language, structure and form contribute to writers' presentation of ideas, themes and settings.

AO3 (for literary heritage poetry)
Make comparisons and explain links between texts, evaluating writers' different ways of expressing meaning and achieving effects.

Writing About Poetry: Develop Your Skills

LEARNING CHECKLIST

This chapter will help you to:

- Recognize what to look for when first responding to a poem.
- Respond with insight and imagination, and select relevant detail from the text to support your interpretations.
- Show understanding of the language features, structure and form a poet chooses.
- Learn how to compare two poems, commenting effectively on links and differences between them.
- Approach your poetry assessments and exams with confidence.

This chapter helps you to practise and develop your skills in writing about any type of poetry. Later in the book, there is a chapter on each poet in the OCR GCSE specifications, so you can focus your attention on the particular poets you are studying. First, you will be equipped with everything you need to practise interpreting and analysing poetry, and to approach and write about all poetry – whether it is by a poet you are studying, or an unseen poem – with confidence.

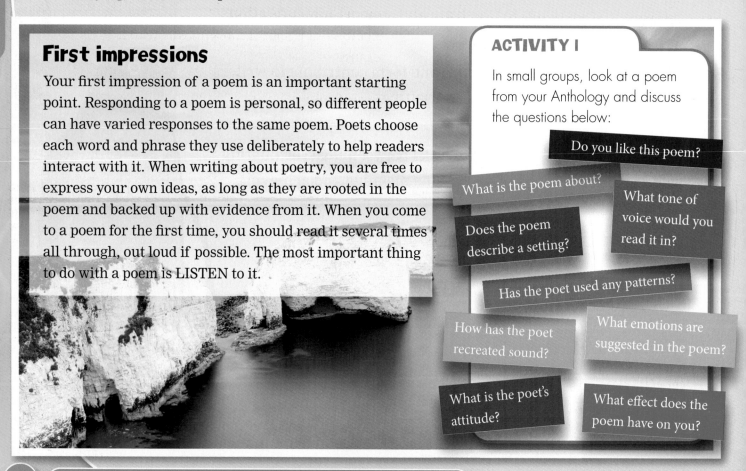

First impressions

Your first impression of a poem is an important starting point. Responding to a poem is personal, so different people can have varied responses to the same poem. Poets choose each word and phrase they use deliberately to help readers interact with it. When writing about poetry, you are free to express your own ideas, as long as they are rooted in the poem and backed up with evidence from it. When you come to a poem for the first time, you should read it several times all through, out loud if possible. The most important thing to do with a poem is LISTEN to it.

ACTIVITY 1

In small groups, look at a poem from your Anthology and discuss the questions below:

Do you like this poem?

What is the poem about?

What tone of voice would you read it in?

Does the poem describe a setting?

Has the poet used any patterns?

How has the poet recreated sound?

What emotions are suggested in the poem?

What is the poet's attitude?

What effect does the poem have on you?

ACTIVITY 2

Now work with a partner. Choose another poem, then working alone, jot down answers to the questions in Activity 1. Compare your responses with your partner's. How are they the same or different? Can you both back up what you are saying with reference to the poem? The discussion will lead you to a fuller appreciation of the poem.

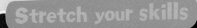

Stretch your skills

Look at two or three different poems which are new to you. Read them over a few times. Underlying the subject of the poem are its themes, which tend to be abstractions, whereas the subject is concrete. What themes are present in your chosen poems? What is the poet saying about those themes? Look closely at the word choices to see how these impressions are created. Write two or three paragraphs on your initial impression of the theme and possible connotations within the text, using evidence from the poems to support your interpretations.

Imagery

Imagery is exactly what it says: an image, captured by the poet and given to you as a picture, to help you see how the poet sees. Poets use imagery to create certain pictures in the minds of their readers. This does not just mean vivid description, but actually comparing one thing to another to help you see it in a new way. Some imagery terms and definitions are shown opposite.

- **metaphor** – a comparison in which one thing becomes another: 'she is my sunshine'
- **personification** – a type of metaphor in which the subject is made into a person: 'the lady moon smiles'
- **simile** – a comparison using 'like' or 'as': 'he ran as fast as a cheetah'
- **symbol** – an object represents an idea: the dove of peace
- **pathetic fallacy** – something emotionless is given feelings: 'the wind wept'

ACTIVITY 3

Copy and complete the grid below, which gives examples from different poems in your Anthology. For each quotation, identify the type of imagery used, and then consider the idea this suggests to the reader. You can look up each poem in your Anthology using the page numbers given.

Quotation	Feature used	Effect created
A moon like an orange drawn by a child (p.157)	Simile	
And the bicycle ticked, ticked, ticked (p.170)		
The slap and plop were obscene threats (p.172)		The frog noises scare the child as though they are trying to warn him to leave them alone.
your tongue a red-hot poker in your throat (p.151)		
I walk on ice, it grimaces, then breaks (p.165)		

ACTIVITY 4

Find some other examples of imagery that appear in the poems in your Anthology. Try to do this with poems that are not by the poet you are studying; looking at unfamiliar poems will mean you may have to work a bit harder to find and understand the imagery used. This is good practice, and will help to sharpen your poetry-analysing skills!

Stretch your skills

Find a photograph of something in nature you find interesting, preferably online, so you can zoom in. Study it and write down as many images as you can think of, using different types of imagery from the list on page 7. Then build on that by considering how it feels to touch, sounds it might make and so on. Share your images with the class, asking them if they can identify what you are describing. Reveal the picture. How accurate do they think your images are? Can they identify the different types? Have your images helped them see your subject more clearly?

Language

Every word of a poem has been chosen carefully and deliberately by the poet to create an effect or to help shape the poem's possible meanings. In addition to visual imagery, poets may use words which emulate sounds, tastes, touch and smell to recreate their experiences so you can participate in them. Poets also use words that make deeper layers of meaning possible, or to build on what words evoke for you. We all enjoy patterns, so sound helps to create the tone. Poems with many rhymes, for example, feel harmonious and confident. Free-verse poems tend to use assonance and consonance, half rhymes and alliteration. Stay tuned!

- **rhyme** – words with similar sounds at their endings: 'sing/ring' (may appear within the lines as well as at the end)
- **onomatopoeia** – words that sound like the thing they describe: 'clatter and clunk'
- **assonance and consonance** – assonance repeats vowel sounds and consonance repeats consonant sounds: 'boozy juice'
- **alliteration** – the same sound is repeated at the start of words close to each other: 'swan swims'
- **connotation** – the different associations words suggest to the reader, beyond the dictionary definition

ACTIVITY 5

You are writing a horrific war poem. Choose the best words to fill in the blanks:

> If in some _____ing dreams you too could _____
> Behind the wagon that we _____ him in,
> And watch the _____ eyes _____ing in his face,
> His hanging face, like a _____ sick of sin;

Compare your choices with Wilfred Owen's (page 67).

- Has he used more precise or interesting words than you?
- Has he found a rhyme for 'face'? Did you?
- Have either of you used words which create alliteration?
- Which version of the poem do you prefer?

ACTIVITY 6

Return to the imagery examples grid on page 8 and add a further column headed 'Language'. What can you add to this column? You may notice some of the devices mentioned above, but also look at the vowel sounds. Are they long or short? What effect does this have on the tone?

For example:

'A moon like an orange drawn by a child' (p.157) is a simile, but also consider the long vowel sounds in 'moon' and 'drawn'. The colour 'orange' suggests warmth. There's also a repetition of 'd'. The line is a soft, lingering one which creates a mood of sweet memories and innocence.

ACTIVITY 7

Choose a poem in your Anthology that is broken up into stanzas and that is by one of the poets you are not studying. Focus on a particular stanza and analyse the language techniques used by the poet here. How does the language chosen suit the subject and help to communicate the ideas?

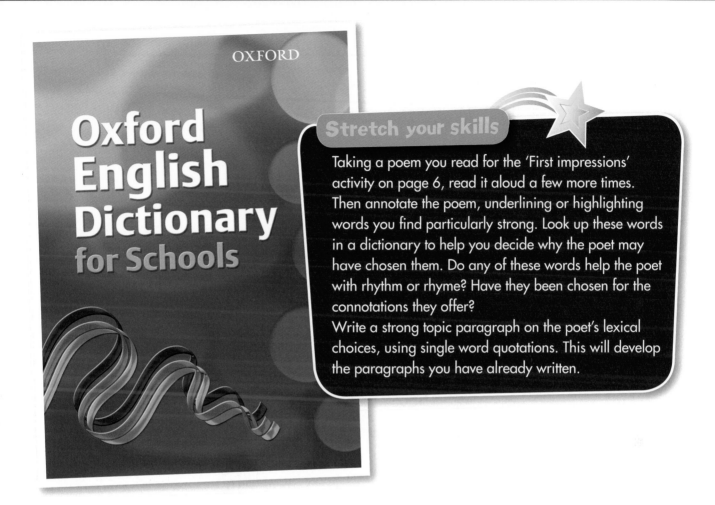

Stretch your skills

Taking a poem you read for the 'First impressions' activity on page 6, read it aloud a few more times. Then annotate the poem, underlining or highlighting words you find particularly strong. Look up these words in a dictionary to help you decide why the poet may have chosen them. Do any of these words help the poet with rhythm or rhyme? Have they been chosen for the connotations they offer?

Write a strong topic paragraph on the poet's lexical choices, using single word quotations. This will develop the paragraphs you have already written.

Structure

Structure is the order of ideas in the poem. Form is the pattern used to shape the poem. Although they are not the same thing, they work together. When looking at the structure of a poem, consider whether the ideas are chronological, or is there a flashback? Why has the poet chosen to start there?

There are many recognized forms, or the poet can invent one. Free verse is a specific type: the poet can have random rhymes or no rhymes at all. Blank verse also has no rhymes, but it has a specific rhythm and line length. The rhythm tends to be more relaxed in free verse, and line breaks indicate little pauses.

Being able to look at the structure of a poem, as well as the form, helps you to get a grip on how the poem as a whole works together and how each part contributes to the main idea. This leads to you being able to access more marks.

ACTIVITY 8

Rhyme scheme

Choose any poem from the Anthology. Label the end sound of the first line **a**, and also any words that rhyme with it as you look down the poem. Label the second sound **b**, and so on. See whether there is a pattern, or a string of different letters. If there is no pattern, it may be free verse.

ACTIVITY 9

Rhythm

When we speak we do not give all syllables the same stress. To find the rhythm, mark all the parts of words that are heavily stressed with a straight line over them. Mark the top of the syllables which are not weighted with a **v**.

For example:

> v   __   v   __   v   __   v   __   v   __
>
> When **for**ty **win**ters **shall** be**siege** thy **brow**

There is a clear pattern here because this is a sonnet written in iambic pentameter. Free verse usually has a pattern that is continually varied throughout the poem.

Find a poem in the Anthology that is in free verse, and one that has a definite 'a-b' rhyme scheme.

- Compare the two poems: what are the different effects of each type of rhyme scheme?
- Try to rewrite a stanza of the free-verse poem so it has an 'a-b' rhyme scheme. How does this change the poem?
- Now change the other poem to free verse.

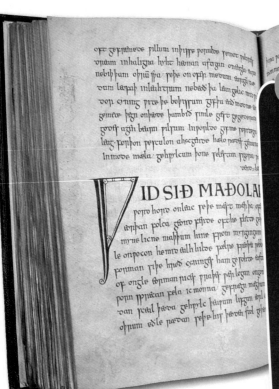

Stretch your skills

There are hundreds of different forms, and poets invent new ones all the time. Research any of the following and see if you can find examples from your own reading of poems from the Anthology: sonnet (both Shakespearean and Petrarchan), quatrain, villanelle, ballad, syllabics, triolet, sestina, free verse.

Caesura: this is a deliberate pause (marked off with a semi-colon or full stop) in a line, often near the centre. It was used heavily in Anglo-Saxon poetry. Look through all the poems you are studying for examples, and explore the effects. Why might the poet have chosen to pause there?

Enjambment: This happens when the lines are run on. In a formal poem this helps the rhyme become more subtle, and should be run on when read. In a free verse poem, however, the line breaks mean a small pause which should be observed when read.

Find some examples in the Anthology to comment on.

Comparison

Comparison is required in your Controlled Assessment, but it is also a very interesting thing to do. Comparing is all about making connections between poems. When choosing which pairing to write about for your Controlled Assessment, consider which one you can see the most links for. You can also look for very subtle links; for example, is similar imagery used? Because you are comparing two poems by the same poet, there may well be stylistic similarities. You are also looking for differences; for example, in approaches to the same subject, different tone of voice, a formal poem and a free verse one on similar topics. When you make comparisons, you discover new things about both poems. Comparing is a creative act.

ACTIVITY 10

Choose two poems from the poet you are studying. Read them carefully. Write down three ways they are similar and three ways they are different. Continue to do this with three or four other possible combinations. This will help you to become more familiar with the poems by your set poet and to become practised at what to look for and comment on when comparing poems.

ACTIVITY 11

Create a master comparison chart across all the poems by your set poet, with the poem titles at the top and the following side headings: subject and theme; imagery; language; structure and form; tone; personal response, including favourite quotes. This should help you see the key differences and similarities between the poems. You can use the grid below to start you off.

	Poem 1	Poem 2	Poem 3	Poem 4	Poem 5 etc..
subject/theme					
imagery					
language					
structure and form					
tone					
personal response					

ACTIVITY 12

Working with a partner, take two poems by your set poet. Giving yourselves about 15 minutes, one of you write down all the similarities between the two poems, and the other write down all the differences between them. Come back together and discuss what you have come up with. Then put together an essay plan that compares the ways in which the poet conveys the central theme of each poem.

Stretch your skills

Take random lines from all the poems by the poet you are studying. Try to arrange them into a collage poem. Create a poster of it for your classroom wall. Challenge your classmates to identify the lines. Doing this exercise will increase your familiarity with the poems, and you will also see which poems fit together best and how style can differ from one to another.

Personal response

Looking at poetry is broken down into different topics so that it is easier to write about. But it is an exercise. It is like stripping down an engine to see how it works. This is fascinating, but unless you put all the parts back together, the engine will not fire. Personal response is where you put the poem back together! Everything in the poem is there for a reason; it helps to communicate the subject and theme of the poem, the poet's point, the shared experience. Personal response is about **you** appreciating the poem, and it is really important to be able to convey effectively **your own response** to a poem in your writing.

SECTION 1

ACTIVITY 13

Choose a poem you like by your set poet.

- What is your favourite word in the poem? Why?
- Is there an image that strikes you as particularly accurate? Quote and explain.
- Is there anything you like about the rhyme, the rhythm or the form?
- Why do you think the poet chose free verse (when applicable)?
- How do all these things help share the message of the poem?

If you like, set out your working in the form of a spider diagram, like the one below:

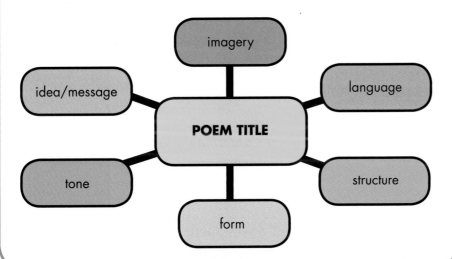

ACTIVITY 14

Make a list of five aspects you like to see in poetry. For example, you might like poems that rhyme, tell a story, make you laugh, etc. Choose five poems by your set poet and award them a mark out of ten for each category. Add up the scores to see which poem you like best. Maybe you will surprise yourself.

Stretch your skills

1) You have decided to make a short film about the poem you like best. Pitch the film to your class, persuading them that the poem you have chosen is the best one to use.

2) Challenge yourself by choosing a poem that is your least favourite, and see what you can find in it to praise.

3) Compose an email that you could send to the poet saying what you like about your favourite poem, and explaining your reasons.

Section 2

Literary Heritage Poets

HOW TO APPROACH THE CONTROLLED ASSESSMENT (FOR ENGLISH LITERATURE)

What do I need to study?

For this part of Unit 1 you will study **either** 15 poems by one poet chosen from the following:

- Robert Browning
- Thomas Hardy
- Wilfred Owen
- Christina Rossetti
- William Shakespeare

or you will study Chaucer's *The General Prologue to the Canterbury Tales*. All of these texts can be found in your *Reflections* Anthology.

How will this unit be assessed?

Literary Heritage Poetry is tested through **Controlled Assessment**. You will write an **extended essay** about two linked poems by the same poet.

Two tasks will be set on each poet and you must respond to **one** of those tasks. The task will ask you to compare two linked, named poems by the poet you have studied. It will contain a list of bullet points, suggesting areas that you should consider in your response.

The tasks will be released by the exam board in June, ready for the assessment in the following January and June. This means you will have plenty of time to think about the tasks and discuss them in the classroom before you write anything. Your teacher will offer advice and guidance.

How much should I write?

For this part of the unit, you will write an extended essay of up to **1000 words** and you will have about **three hours** to complete your writing. This writing time is likely to be split across a number of shorter sessions.

How will my response be marked?

For this task, you will be marked on Assessment Objective 3.

AO3: Make comparisons and explain links between texts, evaluating writers' different ways of expressing meaning and achieving effects. This means that you need to find connections between the two poems and explore them. The connections might include similarities and differences in theme, style, viewpoint and structure.

What are controlled conditions?

When you actually write your response to the task, you must work independently. Before you write it, however, you can think about the task, discuss it in class and make notes on it.

When you write your final response to the task, you will do so under controlled conditions. This means that your work will be closely supervised; you will not be able to communicate with other students or obtain help from your teacher. You will need more than one writing session to complete your response, so you must hand in what you have written at the end of each session; it will then be given back to you at the start of the next lesson.

What can I take into the assessment?

You may take **unannotated** or 'clean' copies of the poems into the Controlled Assessment with you. This means you are **not** allowed to write in the margins of this material during your preparation for the task.

You can also have notes with you when you work on your final version – however, this does not mean you can take in a draft of your essay! It would be wise to keep your notes in an orderly form, organized on a sheet of A4, rather than attempting to work with a huge stack of paper on your desk.

Robert Browning, born in 1812, was brought up in a house of many books. He started writing poetry at an early age. He was educated at home and dropped out of university. At 33, he fell in love with a poet called Elizabeth Barrett, six years his elder and in poor health. They married in secret and went to live in Italy, where her health improved. After her death in 1861, he travelled extensively. He died in 1889 at their son's house in Italy.

ACTIVITY I

For each Browning poem, create a newspaper headline that encapsulates the story it tells. Challenge your class to guess the poem. The results of this activity make an excellent classroom display. Here are some examples:

Duke's plans to remarry plunged into doubt as suspicions grow

(My Last Duchess)

Exiled Poet Longs for Home

(Home-Thoughts, from Abroad)

Mystery man mourns 16-year-old girl's death

(Evelyn Hope)

First impressions

Most of the poems in your Anthology are written using different voices, or personas. They tell a story from one person's viewpoint. The best initial approach to Browning's poems is to read them a few times until you can summarize the narrative into a simple overview.

Browning's poems are often about love, usually love gone wrong, which in some cases leads to murder. He also writes about time and nature. He likes to use different forms, so watch out for his subtle rhymes and strong rhythms. These often influence the pace and flow of the poem.

Choose one of your headlines and create a storyboard for a short film of the events suggested in the poem. If you have access to a video camera, make a film and show it to your class. Or use a digital programme to create a short film using stills and suitable music.

Alternatively, write a newspaper report to develop your headline, or interview some of the characters. 'My Last Duchess', 'The Laboratory' or 'Porphyria's Lover' could be used to role-play a police investigation or a criminal court case.

Imagery

Browning uses imagery sparingly, which can make it all the more effective. It is always an integral part of the poem. 'Home-Thoughts, from Abroad' (page 14) is a lyrical poem that might be expected to include imagery, but in fact relies mostly on precise description. The image of the thrush singing in 'rapture' adds to the mood of happiness. This intensifies the idea of the poet's longing for home.

Browning also draws on personification and the pathetic fallacy, giving feelings to inanimate objects and the weather. This creates a mournful mood in some of his poems.

ACTIVITY 2

Read through all the Browning poems in the Anthology and highlight examples of imagery. Then discuss them with a partner to consider their effect. You will need to read the whole poem carefully to judge this.

Choose three of the images you highlighted in Activity 2 to write about. Follow the example below, and remember to set your ideas in the context of the poem:

In 'Evelyn Hope', Browning compares the hair of the dead girl to 'amber', which makes it sound precious, as amber is a semi-precious stone. Amber also glows and is soft and warm to the touch, which is appropriate for soft shiny hair. 'Amber' is a lovely way to describe red hair and the effect is added to by the comparison of her lips with the red geranium. These vivid colours contrast with the presumed whiteness of the corpse and make her untimely death seem all the more tragic.

Language

Browning is known for his skill in creating vivid descriptions in few words. Look, for example, at 'Meeting at Night' (page 18), which tells of a secret meeting between lovers. The first stanza describes a journey by boat. The use of the word 'startled' to describe the waves shows that the journey is unusual, and the 'mile of warm sea-scented beach' is very evocative of a summer evening. All the sounds in the dark are soft; there is a 'tap' and a 'scratch'. The 'blue spurt of a lighted match' is the only light that pierces the darkness. So much is packed into this 12-line poem!

ACTIVITY 3

Choose a poem, or one section of a long poem. Read it through and underline or highlight any words that surprise you or seem particularly well chosen. Write an appreciation of the poem or section by concentrating on the words you picked out. Don't worry about labelling Browning's techniques – focus on why each word is interesting.

Stretch your skills

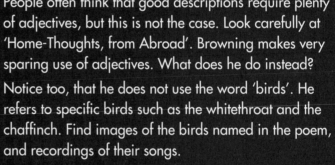

People often think that good descriptions require plenty of adjectives, but this is not the case. Look carefully at 'Home-Thoughts, from Abroad'. Browning makes very sparing use of adjectives. What does he do instead?

Notice too, that he does not use the word 'birds'. He refers to specific birds such as the whitethroat and the chaffinch. Find images of the birds named in the poem, and recordings of their songs.

Structure

Browning uses a straightforward chronological structure for his narrative poems. However, he does sometimes withhold information. For example, in 'How They Brought the Good News from Ghent to Aix', we never discover what the news was. In 'Confessions', the bottle of ether is not really relevant, but is meant to intrigue us. 'My Last Duchess', 'Porphyria's Lover' and 'The Laboratory' end on cliffhangers, as we are not told what happens next.

ACTIVITY 4

Create a grid to analyse the structure of each poem, looking at the order of the ideas. One has been done for you:

Poem title	Structure (order of ideas)	Form
'Now'	Starts by requesting one moment of love, concludes with the moment becoming eternal	Sonnet: 14 lines, unusual interlinked rhyme scheme, ideas developed throughout

Comparison

Your assessment task will ask you to compare two named poems. There will be a choice of two questions. The best way to prepare for the comparison is by looking for links between poems in the selection. For example, 'Home-Thoughts, from Abroad' (page 14) would link well with 'James Lee's Wife III – In the Doorway' (page 17), as one is about the beauty of spring and the other about the sorrows of autumn. Comparing means finding similarities but also differences, which might be in attitude, language, form, mood and so on.

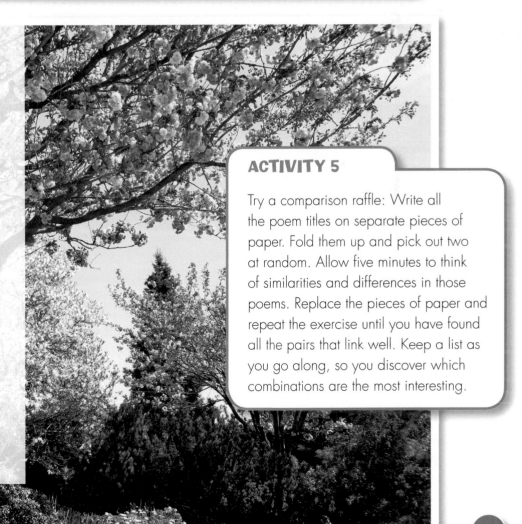

ACTIVITY 5

Try a comparison raffle: Write all the poem titles on separate pieces of paper. Fold them up and pick out two at random. Allow five minutes to think of similarities and differences in those poems. Replace the pieces of paper and repeat the exercise until you have found all the pairs that link well. Keep a list as you go along, so you discover which combinations are the most interesting.

ACTIVITY 6

Choose one of the combinations that worked in Activity 5, and draw up a detailed comparison chart. If other students choose different combinations, you will be able to pool your resources by presenting them in class, possibly as a speaking and listening exercise or assessment.

Use a grid like this for your chart:

	Poem 1 title	Poem 2 title
Subject/theme		
Form and structure		
Mood		
Language		
Attitudes		

Stretch your skills

Try making up your own questions in line with the examples on pages 29–31. Work with a group, and draw up an essay plan for one question. Each group member writes one section of the essay as described in the plan. Then swap sections and annotate the work giving feedback, for example indicating where a quotation has not been included or where a point is too vague. Put the essay together and photocopy it for the group members. Practice makes perfect, and this exercise will help build confidence in your essay-writing skills!

Personal response

Giving a personal response means bringing in your own feelings about a poem. It is about appreciating what you have read. This might involve discussing a word you think is particularly effective, or a character you dislike, a good choice of form, or the way the poem held your interest and made you think. When comparing poems, you may prefer one to another. Giving reasons is crucial; well-expressed personal responses, which give evidence from the poem, can make your essay stand out from the crowd.

ACTIVITY 7

How would you improve this personal response?

'How They Brought the Good News from Ghent to Aix' is an exciting poem about three horsemen galloping from one city to another to tell them some news. The men keep dropping out, which keeps it exciting as it makes me wonder whether any of them will arrive. However, it is annoying that we don't find out what the news actually was.

BROWNING: SAMPLE TASKS

Sample task 1

look at the similarities and differences

using language, form, imagery and character

these are the key words in the question

Poems: 'Evelyn Hope' and 'The Lost Mistress'

Compare the **ways** in which Browning portrays **feelings of loss and rejection** in these poems.

You should consider:

* the **situations** Browning describes

* the **feelings** he portrays

* the **language** he uses.

The bullet points are there to help you address the 'ways' in which Browning works. Don't forget to focus on the actual question; you are being asked to apply it to the named poems, using the bullet points to help you structure your response.

Situations Browning describes

'Evelyn Hope's situation is that the girl he loved is dead, but she never knew of his love. He hopes she will love him in the afterlife.

'The Lost Mistress' has a similar situation in that his love is not returned. But this girl is alive and he at least has her friendship.

Feelings he portrays

The emotions in these two poems are of love and sorrow. These are expressed through descriptions of the surroundings as well as through mood and attitude.

Language he uses

For this bullet point you need to select examples of language which you think are most effective. This is where you can make a big difference to your mark, because you can analyse the style. Include imagery, word choices, rhyme, onomatopoeia and anything else you notice, always relating points back to the situations and feelings shown in the poems.

It is a good idea to make notes on all the poems in the selection using the bullet points, as they remain constant. You can revise using these notes, but the combination of the named poems you are given, and the over-arching question, will give you new ideas. If you know the poems well, any fresh ideas you have will really enhance your work, so don't be afraid to use them.

Sample task 2

look at the similarities and differences

Poems: 'Meeting at Night' and 'Never the Time and Place'

Compare the **ways** in which Browning portrays **passionate secret love** in these poems.

these are the key words in the question

You should consider:

using language, form, imagery and character

- the **situations** Browning describes
- the **feelings** he portrays
- the **language** he uses.

Student response – Sample task 2

bullet points are worked through in order, and signalled in opening sentences

'Meeting at Night' describes a situation where one person has travelled in the dark by sea to meet another secretly. It is a very hushed scene, with whispering and little light, to hide the lovers from anyone spying. 'Never the Time and Place' is different; the lovers can only meet in dreams. Both poems have a happy ending with the secret lovers meeting, but the first poem is real, the second a dream.

words which make comparisons are used, such as 'different', 'both', 'also'

Both poems express passionate feelings. 'Meeting at Night' indicates that the feelings are mutual in the last line: 'two hearts beating each to each'. The lovers are happy to have met but are also terrified in case they are discovered, or perhaps the 'joys and fears' contrast means that the lover in the farm was anxious about the lover travelling on the sea. This poem is very mysterious, which suits the idea of secret love.

key words are repeated to signal relevance

'Never the Time and Place' is also quite mysterious, but the lovers have been unable to find a time and place to meet. It could even be the weather that is keeping them apart as the speaker is very bitter about it, calling it 'hostile' and accusing it of having

Student response – Sample task 2 continued

structure is part of the language bullet point

key words are repeated to signal relevance

'malice'. In this poem, there is only one lover, so we do not know for sure whether the love is returned. The poem begins in sorrow but ends happily when they are together in sleep 'close, safe, warm'. Perhaps the speaker's dreams are enough, or perhaps he is anticipating the day when they can be together: 'This path so soft to pace shall lead/ ... to herself indeed'.

Both poems have an interesting structure which helps to express the passion and secrecy of the love. 'Meeting at Night' has one stanza about the journey and one about the meeting. We do not know until the end of the poem that it is a lovers' tryst. 'Never the Time and Place' has a circular structure; things mentioned near the start such as 'May' and the 'narrow' house are brought in again at the end, but the situation has changed.

language is addressed all through the essay, but there is more to say – this bullet point is the most weighty

EXAMINER'S COMMENTS OCR
RECOGNISING ACHIEVEMENT

- The student switches effectively from one poem to the other in their response, allowing for a fluid comparison.
- Key words from the question are used effectively throughout.
- Quotations are used well throughout to support the student's interpretation.
- There could be further development of the ideas in the final paragraph, but overall this is a good Higher Tier response.

Geoffrey Chaucer

The General Prologue to the Canterbury Tales

Geoffrey Chaucer lived from 1343-1400, and was born into a family of wine dealers. He worked for the King in various important roles, which gave him a chance to travel and meet famous writers. He was married to a lady-in-waiting of the Queen's. He started writing poetry at the age of about 26, and became best known as the writer of *The Canterbury Tales*. No one knows what he died of and some people believe he was murdered. He was the first person to be buried in Poets' Corner in Westminster Abbey.

First impressions

The poem tells the story of a group of pilgrims. They are essentially holiday-makers. Travel in those days was horse-powered and could take a long time, so the pilgrims decide to entertain each other with stories on the way. Don't be put off by the large block of text; it can easily be broken down into sections.

- The first section describes the spring.
- The second tells how the travellers met.
- Most of the poem is taken up with descriptions of all the people going on pilgrimage.
- The last section shows them deciding to travel together.

ACTIVITY I

Skim through, marking off each character, starting with the Knight on page 32 of your Anthology. The beginning of each description is indented and each role is in capitals. Put together a chart with 20 rows, like the one started below.

Character	Physical description	Personality	Quotation
Knight (lines 43-78)	Chain mail, a heavy cotton tunic.	Described (ironically?) as gentle, wise, polite, chivalrous.	'verray, parfit gentil knyght'
Squire (lines 79-100)	Curly hair, good-looking, embroidered clothes, short gown.	A ladies' man, happy, musical, brave.	'He was as fressh as is the month of May'

Using the list of occupations, make another chart, for those jobs which have disappeared from our modern lives. To fill in the third column, you will need to do some research, either on the Internet or in the library.

Occupation	My guess	Fact
Shipman	Someone who build ships?	A ship's captain
Yeoman	A guard at the palace?	A farmer; also a rank in the royal household staff

Chaucer gives us an interesting cast of characters which shows us what it was like to be alive in medieval England. Which job would you most like to have and why?

Imagery

Chaucer aims to describe his characters in a vivid and lively way, so he makes good use of imagery, particularly similes, metaphors, and sometimes personification.

In medieval poetry it was common for nature to be personified, so in the first section, the warm west wind, which the Greeks called Zephyr, is personified: he is spreading his 'sweete breeth' over the countryside to cause spring. The months are also personified. When you are exploring Chaucer's imagery, consider whether he is being approving or disapproving about the character. Comparing someone to something pleasant tends to be positive, whereas a link with something unpleasant can be negative.

ACTIVITY 2

Find the characters that Chaucer describes using these similes and metaphors:

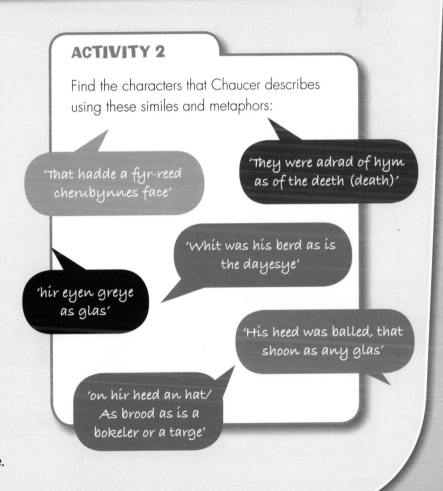

'That hadde a fyr-reed cherubynnes face'

'They were adrad of hym as of the deeth (death)'

'Whit was his berd as is the dayesye'

'hir eyen greye as glas'

'His heed was balled, that shoon as any glas'

'on hir heed an hat/ As brood as is a bokeler or a targe'

Choose a character from Activity 2. Underline the imagery. Then write a few sentences analysing Chaucer's imagery and how it helps him to describe the character.

Example:

> The Somonour (summoner, an usher in a church court) is described as being physically unattractive. His face is 'fyr-reed' and he likes to drink 'strong wyn, reed as blood'. The metaphor and simile relating to the colour red make him sound dangerous. The simile 'lecherous as a sparwe' (sparrow) reduces him to being birdlike, which matches his narrow eyes, and also makes him sound lower than human. On line 642, he is compared to another bird, a jay. When he is drunk he behaves 'as he were wood'. 'Wood' is an old word for 'mad', but it also makes him sound unfeeling and harsh.

Language

There is no need to be daunted by Chaucer's language. Of course, there will be some words you may need to look up in a glossary, but if you read aloud it will be much easier to understand. You will also become used to the strange spellings; for example, **y** and **i** seem to be interchangeable, and **ee** is used instead of **ea**. Make your own list of these oddities as you find them. Some of his spellings are influenced by French, as they are words of French origin that have not yet fully been made part of English; for example, **frère** is 'brother' in French. It means a holy friar.

ACTIVITY 3

Chaucer is very clever at using irony, implying things about characters he wants us to dislike. For example, about the Frere (Friar) he says 'He knew the tavernes wel in every toun', which implies he was a drunkard. Choose one of the following characters and look for examples of irony:

Prioresse   **Millere**   **Monk**   **Frankeleyn**   **Doctour**   **Wif of Bathe**   **Somonour**

See how many French words you can find in the poem, and list them. Use a French dictionary to find out meanings. Do they mean the same in English?

French	English
visage	face

Stretch your skills

Choose one or two of the characters. Look closely at the language Chaucer uses. Make notes on:

- Colour
- Rhyme
- Humour
- Irony

Swap notes with a partner who has worked on a different character. Using each other's notes, produce a paragraph exploring the way the character is presented. Then, working together from the two paragraphs, bring them together in a point by point comparison.

ACTIVITY 4

Chaucer uses rhyming couplets all the way through this poem. This helps to hold the poem together and sometimes can produce humour, as very different things can be connected by the rhyme. Choose a small section of about 10 lines and explore the effect of the rhymes. Are any of them surprising?

Structure

In 'First impressions' we looked at the overall structure of the character descriptions being framed by the narrative sections. But in what order does Chaucer introduce the characters, and why? Does he group any together, and why? Does he contrast them by juxtaposition (placing them next to very different ones)? Chaucer may have been influenced by the fact that he intended each character to tell a story. Is the order of the characters going to make for a suitable variety in the tales?

ACTIVITY 5

Chaucer writes his prologue in iambic pentameter, the same type of line length and metre that Shakespeare uses for his plays and sonnets. Revisit the section you looked at for rhyme in Activity 4. Highlight the places where the stressed syllables fall. You should be able to see that, mostly, the pattern is an unstressed syllable followed by a stressed one. What are the effects of using a strong rhythm, and why this rhythm in particular?

Stretch your skills

Sort the characters into class types using the following boxes:

Military	Clergy	Upper middle class	Lower middle class	Villagers	Church officers
Knight Squire Yeoman					

There are no noble characters as they would have travelled separately. Peasants would not have been able to go on holiday as they had to work every day. Is the order the characters are introduced in connected with the class structure of the times? Has Chaucer grouped them according to profession? Why might this seem natural? Why are there so few women?

Comparison

In your Controlled Assessment, you will be asked to compare two characters and will be given the lines where their descriptions are located. You will be asked to write about:

- the appearance and personality of each character
- how Chaucer makes you feel about each character
- the language he uses.

The best way to do this is to work through the bullet points, looking at BOTH the characters under each heading, and making connections between them, both in similarities and differences.

Do take time to plan, using a quick comparison chart.

Character 1	Character 2

To write your essay, work across your chart. Use very brief quotations for evidence.

ACTIVITY 6

To practise for the assessment:

- work with a partner to pair characters up
- each take responsibility for looking at the bullet-point responses for one character
- together, look for similarities and differences between the characters.

Personal response

Poetry is all about the poet wanting to communicate with readers. Your personal response really matters. Chaucer wrote this poem a long time ago, which makes the language tricky to understand until you are used to it. However, he did write to entertain, and the poem is still read for pleasure today. It is also valued as a portrait of medieval society. People enjoy Chaucer's wit and his unflinching descriptions of characters from all walks of life. Personal response is all about explaining what you think is particularly successful about the work you are considering.

ACTIVITY 7

Looking back, which three character descriptions appeal to you the most and why? Look again at the lines which deal with these three. Imagine you have been given the job of selecting phrases for a picture book version of 'The General Prologue'. List the ones you would choose, then write a sentence or two about why that phrase appeals.

Example:

The Wife of Bath wears shoes that are 'ful moyste and newe'.

This is a good phrase because it shows how rich and vain she is, as she can afford new shoes, and the fact that the leather was flexible and soft indicates she can afford the best and that fashion is important to her. This is a clever way for Chaucer to show what is important to her, and fits in well with the size of her hat, which again shows her status.

The highlighted phrases show personal response.

Sample task I

> Answer ONLY on the named characters. Marks will not be given for points on others.

- *Lines 445–476: the description of the Wife of Bath*
- *Lines 545–566: the description of the Miller.*

Compare the **ways** in which Chaucer **portrays the Wife of Bath and the Miller** in 'The General Prologue'.

> Focus on THE WAYS or methods that Chaucer uses, such as rhythm, rhyme, imagery etc.

You should consider:

- the physical appearance and personality of each character
- how Chaucer makes you feel about each character
- the language he uses.

> Bullet points help you structure your answer but they are not the question.

As demonstrated above, it is important to PLAN your response. This is the best way to ensure you answer the question set. When you see the question, follow these steps to success:

1. Identify the passages in your clean copy and rule them off at both ends.
2. Re-read both passages carefully.
3. Re-read the question. The bullet points are there to give you some ideas, so use them, but don't feel limited by them.
4. Re-read the passages looking for points you want to make.
5. Write a quick plan as a comparison chart:

	The Wife of Bath	**The Miller**
Imagery	Big hat/like a shield	Sow's ears – piglike man
Irony	Lines 449-450	Gold thumb image is ironic
Form and structure	Juxtaposition of lines 459/460 – humour	Starts with a description of how big he is, ends with how noisy he is

6. Include any similarities and differences between the characters, such as in this case: they are from different social spheres but both involved in trade; they are both physically impressive but the Miller is ugly and the Wife is attractive. Do this in note form.
7. Another way to plan might be a quick mindmap. Use the main categories for WAYS and give each one two branches, one for each character.
8. It does not matter HOW you plan, but it is vital that you DO plan.
9. Dive straight in and start comparing straight away, always remembering to talk about WAYS. The best opening paragraphs tackle the question straight away and give an overview.
10. Stay on track by following your plan. Stick to the two characters you have been asked to compare.

Sample task 2

The key word in the question is WAYS again. This word invites you to analyse.

- *Lines 118–162: the description of the Prioress*
- *Lines 208–269: the description of the Friar*

Compare the **ways** in which Chaucer **portrays the Prioress and the Friar** in 'The General Prologue'.

The Prioress is higher class than the Friar, and a nicer person too.

You should consider:

- the physical appearance and personality of each character
- how Chaucer makes you feel about each character
- the language he uses.

Having different characters to look at will give you different comparison points. You will always be given characters that compare well. These two are both clergy.

Student response – Sample task 2

the student starts by comparing and giving an overview of WAYS, such as physical attractiveness

several carefully observed details have been chosen to illustrate points

The Prioress and the Friar are **both** clergy, but the Prioress is a higher class. Chaucer uses several ways to bring them to life, such as detailed physical descriptions, imagery, examples of their behaviour, irony and humour.

The physical descriptions of the characters are very telling. The Prioress is very pretty, with a high forehead 'almoost a spanne brood' which is a mark of her intelligence and class. She has a small, well-formed 'tretys' nose and a 'coy' smile, which implies she pretends to be shy. She is careful her wimple is nicely pinned to flatter her face: 'Ful semyly hir wympul pynched was', and even her name, Madame Eglentyne, which means wild rose, is used to suggest how sweet and lovely she is. Her eyes are 'greye as glas', very expensive then. The 'g' alliteration emphasizes the soft colour grey.

notice use of comparison words like 'neither', 'both', etc.

short quotations are woven seamlessly into the essay and support the student's descriptions

Student response – Sample task 2 continued

details are packed in without any waffle

notice use of comparison words like 'neither', 'both', etc.

look at how the ways have been pointed out as comparisons are made

evidence has been brought together from different parts of the text

The Friar is also attractive. His neck is white, which shows he is clean. It is compared to 'flour-de-lys', which is very noble as it was used on coats of arms. He wears a smart half cloak, which is made of a better cloth than friars normally had. He speaks with a lisp, which Chaucer implies is put on: 'To make his Englissh sweete upon his tonge'. He also has twinkling eyes. His name, Huberd, derives from 'hug' and 'bright', which seems very apt as he seduces women.

Neither the Prioress nor the Friar is holy. The Prioress wears jewellery and her gold brooch has a Latin motto which means 'love conquers all', suggesting she has been in love at some time. However, the Friar is much worse. Chaucer's irony implies that the Friar seduces women all the time. By using words like 'daliaunce', 'famulier... with worthy wommen', and 'wantownesse', Chaucer shows him flirting with every woman he meets. He even carries little presents to give to women. He is very fond of money and seems to be able to gain it from people all the time: 'Men moote yeve silver to the povre freres', possibly in exchange for hearing their confession and other favours. Both the Prioress and the Friar are very interested in possessions, but the Friar is dishonest and selfish.

notice that one or two examples are enough to show skills

the essay is rooted in the text and keeps going back to it

EXAMINER'S COMMENTS OCR

- This is an excellent response; it is focused and perceptive and rooted firmly in the text.
- The student moves smoothly from descriptions and interpretations of the Prioress and the Friar, using one or two examples for each point and backing them up with textual evidence.
- Both short and longer quotations from the text are used effectively.

Thomas Hardy

Thomas Hardy was born in 1840 and lived in Dorset. He married Emma Gifford in 1874. He achieved fame as a novelist first and also wrote many short stories. He always said his first love was poetry and he wrote several volumes in his later years. Hardy's work is very autobiographical as he used events from his own life in his poems. Emma died in 1912 and Hardy remarried in 1914. He died in 1928.

First impressions

Your first impression, reading the titles, may well be that Hardy's poems are about rather abstract ideas or that they are concerned with people, places and animals. You would be correct in both because he uses events in his life and the nature around him to try and make sense of the universe. Several of the poems are about Emma or her family. Some are about war or about love and death. Others are about faith and hope in an uncaring world. What they all have in common is a care for humanity and for the natural world.

Photo London Stereo

Imagery

Hardy's images can be powerful, summing up a whole feeling in a well-chosen phrase, like 'time-torn man' (in 'A Broken Appointment') which can mean several things all at once. It calls up a picture of a man restlessly pacing, torn between waiting and going, and one to whom time has been unkind. The connotations of being torn by time are violent. Hardy also uses images of nature to describe places he knows well or those he can only imagine. He uses the senses as well as weather, colours and personification to draw the reader in. He uses words that are exact and economical.

SECTION 2

ACTIVITY 2

Work with a partner and group the images opposite under suitable headings, such as 'places', 'weather', 'senses', 'colours', 'personification', etc. Some may fit under more than one heading.

'cleaving wing' (p.57)

'Frost was spectre-gray' (p.59)

'an irised rain' (p.53)

'its slope, now glistening wet' (p.52)

'strange-eyed constellations' (p.51)

'lamplight's yellow glance' (p.54)

'hope-hour' (p.51)

'spudding up docks' (p.62)

Stretch your skills

Work with a partner and examine each poem in turn. Select images from each poem that you consider to be effective. Then create a grid like the one below for each poem. There is an example to get you started.

Poem title	Image in quotation	What the image means	Why the image is effective
The Voice	'the original air-blue gown'	Hardy imagines Emma as he first met her, in the same dress which is described as 'air-blue' like the sky on a clear day.	It associates Emma with bright days of the past, now she is no longer there.

Language

Hardy's poetic language is varied and covers local dialect, abstract ideas and some archaic or unusual words such as 'twain' for two. 'Wessex' is the name he used for the south-west of England and his local poems use the Dorset dialect. From his atheism come terms such as 'Immanent Will' that he uses to describe the force behind fate or the working of the universe. His archaic words suggest timelessness connecting past and present, appropriate since time is one of his main themes. He is fond of hyphenated adjectives such as 'strange-eyed' or 'blast-beruffled' and sound patterning is a favourite technique.

ACTIVITY 3

Copy the poems 'The Oxen' and 'The Ruined Maid'.

- Highlight the dialect words and phrases in each poem.
- Use some of these to write an imaginary conversation between the village elder in 'The Oxen' and the narrator in 'The Ruined Maid'.
- Write a paragraph about the effects of Hardy's use of local dialect on character, situation and feeling.

Study the poem 'The Convergence of the Twain':

- find three quotations that suggest fallen vanity
- find three quotations to do with the Titanic's construction
- find three quotations that show the iceberg's growth
- find three quotations about the meeting of the ship and the iceberg.

Discuss the feelings in the poem. Why is there no mention of the passengers or crew? What words and phrases does Hardy use to suggest that fate and human vanity played a part in the accident?

Write an article for the Internet site 'suite101. com' about Hardy's use of language in this poem.

Structure

Hardy uses different structures in his poems according to the subject. For example in 'The Convergence of the Twain' his three-line stanzas resemble a ship, while in 'Beeny Cliff' the lines are long and even. Both 'Drummer Hodge' and 'Transformations' have three six-line stanzas and they have a similar theme. In 'The Ruined Maid' the form is a conversation, while in 'During Wind and Rain' the final two lines of each stanza seem to reverse the mood of the previous five lines. Most of his poems contain rhymes and use rhythms appropriate to their themes and ideas.

ACTIVITY 4

Work with a partner to complete the grid for every poem.

Poem Title	Rhyme	Rhythm	Time scheme
In Time of 'The Breaking of Nations'			A few minutes' observation, but refers to centuries past and future.
The Oxen	Alternate rhyming lines give simplicity, like memories of childhood		
The Darkling Thrush		Hardy uses ballad metre to write about despair and hope	

Comparison

You can compare Hardy's poems through subject matter, characters, situation, feelings or language. There are several poems about his first wife Emma. Many of the poems are about time, war, nature, transformation and fate. Love, loss, disappointment, and care for nature are among the feelings Hardy shows. There is also humour in some of the poems, along with comment on his society. The poems are mainly in simple or straightforward words, but Hardy sometimes uses compound words, such as 'lovingkindness' to express a concept. Situations in his poems include memories, people and nature, moments of 'seeing' and meetings of various kinds.

ACTIVITY 5

Use copies of 'Drummer Hodge' on page 51, and the two poems on page 56 of your Anthology. Work with a partner to annotate the poems looking at:

- what each of them says about war
- the characters and situation in each one
- the language and structure
- ideas of time and change.

One person writes about similarities, the other about differences. Compare findings.

ACTIVITY 6

Use copies of the poems on pages 52, 53, 60 and 'The Voice' on page 63 of your Anthology. Work with a partner to annotate the poems. Then use a spider diagram to make comparisons.

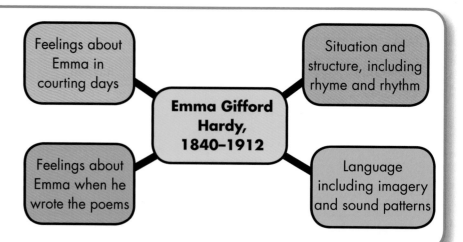

Feelings about Emma in courting days

Situation and structure, including rhyme and rhythm

Emma Gifford Hardy, 1840–1912

Feelings about Emma when he wrote the poems

Language including imagery and sound patterns

Stretch your skills

Work with a partner to prepare a PowerPoint presentation comparing one of the following pairs of poems:

- 'A Broken Appointment' and 'Beyond the Last Lamp'
- 'The Darkling Thrush' and 'The Oxen'
- 'The Ruined Maid' and 'Transformations'
- 'During Wind and Rain' and 'The Convergence of the Twain'

Your slides should include similarities and differences in:

- subject matter
- characters
- feelings
- situation
- language
- structure.

Remember to include quotations to support your points – you could put these in speech bubbles. You can also use colour, pictures, music and shape boxes to enhance your presentation.

Personal response

One of the criticisms that people make of Hardy's poetry is that it is too pessimistic. Hardy said 'It is the only view of life in which you can never be disappointed.' Other people have found a surprising optimism in his poems. He seems very aware of his own failings, but shows humanity to others. He is a critic of his society and its intolerance. Hardy thought that 'the relations of the sexes' should be honestly portrayed, since they were important. These are things to consider when judging your response to what Hardy says and how he says it.

ACTIVITY 7

Make a YouTube video of one of Hardy's poems from the Anthology. Choose one poem to interpret and put together a reading of the poem with pictures and/or music that you think would help the viewer to understand the poem. It can be simple or technically complex. Upload it to YouTube when it's finished.

HARDY: SAMPLE TASKS

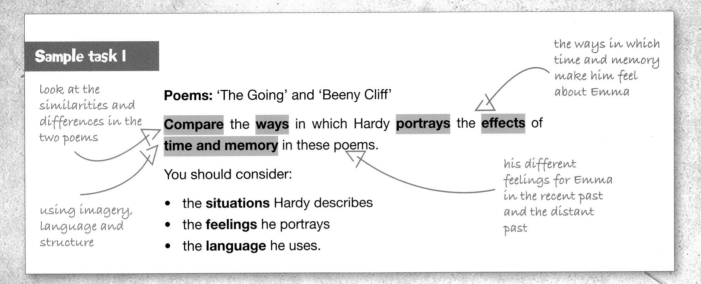

Sample task 1

look at the similarities and differences in the two poems

Poems: 'The Going' and 'Beeny Cliff'

the ways in which time and memory make him feel about Emma

Compare the **ways** in which Hardy **portrays** the **effects** of **time and memory** in these poems.

You should consider:

using imagery, language and structure

his different feelings for Emma in the recent past and the distant past

- the **situations** Hardy describes
- the **feelings** he portrays
- the **language** he uses.

1. You could add further boxes with short quotations to this spider diagram:

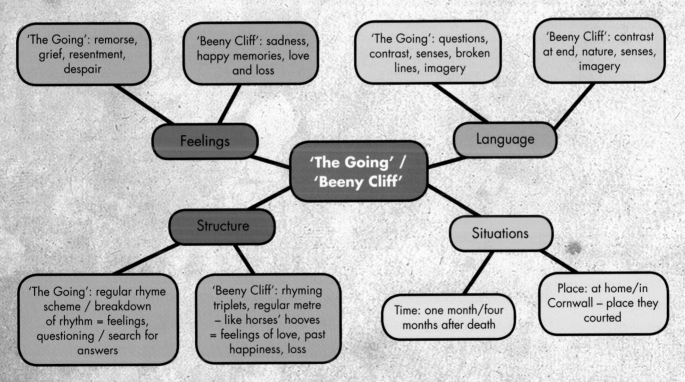

'The Going': remorse, grief, resentment, despair

'Beeny Cliff': sadness, happy memories, love and loss

'The Going': questions, contrast, senses, broken lines, imagery

'Beeny Cliff': contrast at end, nature, senses, imagery

Feelings

Language

'The Going' / 'Beeny Cliff'

Structure

Situations

'The Going': regular rhyme scheme / breakdown of rhythm = feelings, questioning / search for answers

'Beeny Cliff': rhyming triplets, regular metre – like horses' hooves = feelings of love, past happiness, loss

Time: one month/four months after death

Place: at home/in Cornwall – place they courted

2. Plan your answer based on parts of the question – time and memory, how the reader is made aware of situation, feelings and language in each poem and how these are similar and different. Make sure you select appropriate quotations and embed them in your answer as evidence. An example of a plan is shown on the next page.

Opening

- situation relating to time and memory

Development

- look at structure of 'The Going' – relate to time and memory
- comment on feelings as shown in language (including imagery) – relate to time and memory

Comparison

- look at structure of 'Beeny Cliff' – relate to time and memory
- compare/contrast with 'The Going'
- comment on feelings as shown in language (including imagery) – relate to time and memory and compare/contrast

Conclusion

- difference made to time and memory by situation.

Sample task 2

look at similarities and differences

for one person or for both people

Poems: 'A Broken Appointment' and 'Beyond the Last Lamp'

Compare the **ways** in which Hardy presents **disappointments** in **relationships** in these two poems.

You should consider:

using imagery, structure and language

- the **situations** Hardy describes
- the **feelings** he portrays
- the **language** he uses.

think about the kind of relationships shown and what feelings may exist between the people in the poems

---

Student response – Sample task 1

use of dates to establish time

'The Going' was written just a month after Emma's death, when her memory is still fresh and tinged with the estrangement that afflicted their relationship in later years. Time has not yet begun

evidence of research

to work its healing power as it has in 'Beeny Cliff', written three months later when Hardy re-visited the scenes of their courtship.

good brief overview to open

In 'The Going' Hardy has used a regular rhyme scheme and

evidence of research

metre to impose order on his emotions, but these break down

valid comment on use of structure to convey meaning

towards the end when he describes himself as 'a dead man held on end'. His feelings of grief are made stronger because Emma 'gave

Student response – Sample task I continued

valid interpretation of mood

no hint' that she would die. His initial feelings seem to be of resentment that she could go and never 'lip me the softest call'.

apt quotations embedded fluently in the writing

The poem begins with 'Why' as do the third and fifth stanzas. This is an unanswerable question. Hardy's grief is made more unbearable by guilt at his treatment of Emma in the question 'Why, then, latterly did we not speak' and his sudden realization

sound evaluation of evidence

of how much she had meant to him. The phrase 'up and be gone', which implies a deliberate desertion, gives way to 'your great going', suggesting a momentous event which 'altered all.'

apt quotations embedded fluently in the writing

understanding of Hardy's technique

In 'Beeny Cliff' the rhythm of the rhyming triplets echoes the sound of the waves breaking on the shore below, as well as the sound of the horse's hooves galloping across the top, ridden by Emma with her 'bright hair flapping free'. The scene, full of colour and life, and the young Emma on her pony are merged

imaginative and well-founded interpretation

through a sense of freedom tinged with wildness. The memories here are vivid, 'opal and sapphire' of the sea and sky and 'purples prinked the main' of the shadowed Atlantic.

well selected quotations

good comparison

This time when they 'laughed light-heartedly' holds no bitterness or resentment, unlike 'The Going', but it creates a great sadness for the memory that she 'will laugh there nevermore'. While the ending provides a contrast to their courting days, in 'Beeny Cliff' there is no breakdown within the lines, just a parenthesis round '– elsewhere –' that implies an absence.

effective contrast and good use of detail

EXAMINER'S COMMENTS OCR

- The student provides a strong opening paragraph with context for both poems and evidence of research, but without losing focus on the question.
- Perceptive interpretations of the poet's language choices and mood are offered. These are backed up with sound evidence from both poems.
- This is an extremely good answer, doing as much as could be reasonably demanded under exam conditions.

Wilfred Owen

Wilfred Owen was born in 1893. He joined up to fight in the First World War and was sent to France as a Second Lieutenant at the end of 1916. After suffering shell shock, he was sent to Craiglockhart Hospital where he met Siegfried Sassoon, who helped him with his writing. He returned to France and was killed in action, aged 25, a week before the Armistice. He was posthumously awarded the Military Cross for gallantry.

First impressions

Owen's poems seem to combine romanticism and realism. His poems tell of the horror of war, but also of the suffering of the men, who are sometimes seen in a religious light as Christ's representatives and usually as innocent victims of the conflict created by people in power. The poems tell of the soldiers' appalling injuries – mental and physical – and the terrible conditions they had to endure. Some are written in the voices of the men themselves, others are distanced and abstract. It is always possible to sense Owen's experience as an officer in the front lines.

ACTIVITY I

Work with a partner. Take the first line of each poem and put them on one page together. Now rearrange the lines into a poem of your own.

Discuss what your poem is saying about war and what clues it gives you to Owen's themes and ideas in these poems. Compare your poem with others in the class.

Stretch your skills

Work with a partner and listen to readings of Owen's poems. You can find some of them online at YouTube and Eaglesweb.com. As you listen, make notes on a grid like the one below.

Poem title	Strong words or images	Rhyme and metre
Anthem for Doomed Youth	Monstrous anger	
Conscious		Alternate rhyming lines, iambic pentameter

When you have completed your grid, compare it with other pairs of students. Discuss any similarities or differences in your choices. Decide if you wish to amend your grid.

Write a paragraph saying what you have learned about Owen's poems through listening to them.

SECTION 2

Imagery

Owen is noted for his use of precise images that convey the situation and feelings of men in extreme conditions, whether they are burying or remembering comrades, suffering from injuries or trying to protect themselves from severe weather. His comparisons are memorable. From the 'demented choirs' of shells (page 64) to 'purgatorial shadows' (page 70) to 'Eyeballs, huge-bulged like squids'' (page 78) he uses connotations that echo the horror and pity of war and its effects on ordinary men. They can be universal, as in 'granites which titanic wars had groined' (page 72) or personal, as in 'He's wounded, killed and pris'ner all the lot' (page 75).

ACTIVITY 2

Use a copy of 'Dulce et Decorum Est'. Highlight the following:

- three phrases that describe the men's condition before the attack
- three phrases that describe the man failing to fit his gas mask
- three phrases that describe his condition in the wagon.

Imagine you are the narrator. Write the entry in your diary, describing this event and using your highlighted phrases.

Stretch your skills

Look at 'The Sentry' and work with a partner. Imagine this event forms a scene in a new film you are directing about Wilfred Owen. You need to create the following:

- a storyboard showing stills that will represent each section
- a sound track, including the armaments mentioned
- a script including dialogue and actions
- music to heighten the tension and point up the action
- a cast list for the scene, including the actors who will play the roles
- a labelled design for the set on which the scene will be filmed.

Language

Owen's language ranges from the elevated diction of 'Strange Meeting', where 'nations trek from progress', through figurative language, such as 'Voices of boys rang saddening like a hymn' (page 65), to the colloquial: 'I'm in the pink at present, dear' (page 75). This enables him to present a variety of viewpoints, from the historic and abstract to the immediate and personal. He never flinches from showing the horror of war, as in 'white eyes writhing' (page 67) and 'jaws that slob their relish' (page 70); describing the terror of an attack, as in 'Breasted the surf of bullets' (page 72); showing the sheer boredom, as in 'But nothing happens' (page 68); and revealing the lack of glory: 'creep back, silent' (page 77).

ACTIVITY 3

Look at the poem 'The Dead-Beat' with a partner. Highlight the following:

- words and phrases that describe the dead-beat
- Owen's use of pronouns
- words and phrases that show the attitude of the other men
- words and phrases that suggest his true condition
- Owen's use of irony.

Write a paragraph on Owen's use of language in this poem.

Stretch your skills

Look at the two poems 'The Chances' and 'The Letter'.

- Work with a partner and make a list of the slang and colloquial terms in each one and find out what they mean.
- Write a monologue in role as Jim in 'The Letter' saying what happened and how you came to be writing to the narrator's wife (you will have to give the narrator a name). Use the language that Owen gives the men in these poems.
- Then, still in role as Jim, write the letter to the narrator's wife that was his last request to you.

Structure

Owen uses a variety of forms in his poetry, from the sonnet to longer narrative and blank verse. His rhyme schemes are carefully thought out, whether he is using full rhymes, half rhymes (consonance on the final consonants, as in *once* and *France*), or pararhymes (where all the consonants are the same, but the vowels aren't, as in *burn* and *born*). Sometimes rhymes are linked across stanzas. In 'Mental Cases' the absence of regular rhymes reinforces the lack of order and reason. 'The Send-Off' uses short stanzas that seem to express separate thoughts or rumours. The structure of each poem differs according to its subject; notice, for example, the uneven stanza lengths of 'Dulce et Decorum Est', the repetition in the final lines of each stanza in 'Exposure', and Owen's use of the ellipsis (…) to show fragmented thoughts in 'Conscious'.

ACTIVITY 4

Answer the following questions about the poem 'The Chances':

a What is the subject of each stanza?

b Why is the rhyme scheme different for the final four lines?

c Why has Owen used iambic pentameter (see page 12) as his metre?

d What happens between the beginning of the poem and the end?

Write a paragraph about Owen's use of structure in this poem.

Stretch your skills

Copy the poem 'Spring Offensive' and work with a partner to do the following:

- use a pencil to link the rhyming words
- discuss what is interesting about Owen's use of rhyme
- discuss and make notes about the use of time and place throughout the poem
- discuss the movement and activity in the poem – how might it reflect the war as a whole?
- summarize what happens in the poem in three sentences.

Write two or three paragraphs describing how the structure of this poem helps the reader to understand its meaning.

Comparison

The obvious comparison is that these poems are all about war, but the situations, feelings and language are all different. Owen has used individuals in poems such as 'The Sentry' and 'Disabled' to show how war affects a man. The feelings he evokes range from anger and disgust, as in 'Dulce et Decorum Est', to the pity and love shown in 'Futility'. His soldiers are in a variety of situations, ranging from mental hospitals in 'Mental Cases', through the trenches as in 'The Dead-Beat', to the after-life of 'Strange Meeting'. His language is both archaic and contemporary; descriptive and colloquial; abstract and gut-wrenchingly real.

ACTIVITY 5

Work with a partner and look at 'The Dead-Beat' and 'The Sentry'. On paper, draw four boxes for each poem with the same headings as the ones below.

Characters **Situations** **Feelings** **Language**

In each box, write a list of ideas that relate to the headings. Then compare the lists you have made for each poem and highlight similarities and differences.

ACTIVITY 6

Work with a partner and look at 'Disabled' and 'Dulce et Decorum Est'. Design a poster to help other students reading these poems. Use the following:

- pictures of the characters in the two poems
- comments about feelings, in square speech bubbles
- comments about situations, in round speech bubbles
- comments about language, in thought bubbles
- quotations showing similarities, in one colour
- quotations showing differences, in another colour.

Stretch your skills

Work with a partner and look at 'The Send-Off' and 'Anthem for Doomed Youth'. Design a PowerPoint presentation to compare these two poems in terms of:

- characters and subject matter
- feelings and emotions
- situations – in different locations
- language – including imagery and techniques
- structure – including rhyme scheme, metre, time scale and narrative.

You should use quotations, perhaps in speech bubbles, to support your points. Include relevant pictures, use colours and shapes for your text, and add music. Suitable pictures and songs can be found at firstworldwar.com and similar sites.

Personal response

Wilfred Owen's poems were shocking when they were written and they are still shocking now. He does not spare his readers the gruesome details of the effects of war on human beings. You may find the poems interesting because of their often anti-war message or because of what they say about human resilience. Often the poems are written from his personal viewpoint as an officer, or he uses the voices of his men. Owen's language mixes the slang of the trenches with descriptions so vivid that they live with you afterwards. You may, and you should, find his poems troubling.

ACTIVITY 7

Choose one of Owen's poems. Make a short film showing your view of it, using:

- a storyboard with captions showing pictures in order
- a script with narrative and actions
- a reading of the poem with appropriate pictures/music.

When you are ready, put it together on a computer. You can use a webcam or ask a partner to film it.

OWEN: SAMPLE TASKS

shelter, weather, boredom, protection, defence against weapons, clothes, etc.

Sample task I

look at the similarities and differences

using imagery, language and structure

Poems: 'Exposure' and 'Spring Offensive'

Compare the **ways** in which Owen portrays the **conditions** in which the soldiers fought the war in these poems.

You should consider:

- the **situations** Owen describes

- the **feelings** he portrays

- the **language** he uses.

A A list of things to include in your answer, including appropriate short quotations

Situation
Weather – winter, 'merciless iced east winds', versus spring, 'summer oozed into their veins'
Danger – winter rain and snow more dangerous than bullets, versus attacking into shell and machine-gun fire
Protection – no shelter from freezing weather, versus no shelter from guns and shells, both 'exposed'

Feelings
Boredom – 'nothing happens', versus anticipation: waiting for signal to attack, 'come to the end of the world'
Despair – 'on us the doors are closed', versus excitement, 'a lift and flare of eyes'

Misery – 'We cringe in holes', versus terror, 'hot blast and fury of hell's upsurge'

Language
First person –'Our brains ache', immediate and personal, versus third person, 'Sharp on their souls', more detached observer
Use of alliteration, especially sibilants, to imitate weather (often onomatopoeic), versus use of contrast before, during and after battle
Images of nature as enemy, versus images of nature as friend being destroyed like men

Structure
Consistent rhyme scheme across stanzas and repetition creating continuity, versus variations in stanzas breaking poem into incidents

B A planned outline

Introduction, giving situation in each poem briefly
Comparison of situations looking at weather, activity and lack of protection/shelter in each poem, with supporting quotations and explanations

Comparison of feelings in each poem with supporting quotations and explanations
Comparison of language use in each poem, commenting on its effectiveness
Conclusion, looking at how structure helps meaning in each poem.

Sample task 2

look at the similarities and differences

using imagery, language and structure

Poems: 'The Letter' and 'The Send-Off'

Compare how Owen shows the differences between the **soldiers at war** and **the people at home** in these poems.

those on the front lines or going to war

You should consider:

- the **situations** Owen describes
- the **feelings** he portrays
- the **language** he uses.

wives and families and other civilians safe in England

Student response – Sample task 1

starts straight into the question, comparing the situations in a brief overview

In 'Exposure' Owen shows the hardships of the men in the trenches during the winter when 'the merciless east winds that knive us' are like the enemy. In 'Spring Offensive' the weather is warm and nature is friendly with buttercups under their boots, but the enemy is waiting to mow them down. In the first poem they are exposed to the cold and in the second to enemy fire, described as 'the whole sky burned/ With fury' which shows how many bullets and shells are filling the air around them.

appropriate and embedded quotations used

perceptive points about feelings with supporting evidence and evaluation

Owen shows that the men in 'Exposure' feel despairing about their survival because he says 'our ghosts drag home' and 'We turn back to our dying' which implies that they think they will never arrive back home as living men. The only thing that keeps them there is the belief that their suffering is the only way 'kind fires burn' which is a way of saying that their homes and families will be safe.

well-chosen quotations to support comments on feelings

In 'Spring Offensive' the men are excited, anticipating the order to attack. I know this because Owen describes 'a lift and

SECTION 2

Student response – Sample task I continued

flare of eyes' which shows they are alert and waiting to go. This is a contrast with how they are shown after the battle when those who survived 'speak not... of comrades that went under'.

quotation needs more evaluation

well-chosen quotations to support comments on feelings

The language Owen uses is very descriptive. In 'Exposure' dawn is described in terms of an enemy 'massing in the east her melancholy army' which suggests that nature is more of an enemy than the Germans. When an attack does come the bullets are seen as 'Less deathly than the air that shudders black with snow'. The men know they are more likely to die from hypothermia than enemy gunfire.

thoughtful points about language use, well explained

The opposite is true for the soldiers in 'Spring Offensive' as they are safe in 'the warm field / And the far valley behind' but when they have to attack they 'Breasted the surf of bullets', a metaphor that compares them to swimmers wading through waves of deadly gunfire.

clear points of comparison with first poem

use of correct technical terms

EXAMINER'S COMMENTS OCR

- The student has engaged imaginatively with the poems and offers a perceptive personal response to Owen's writing.
- Interpretations are supported with apt quotations from the text.
- This is a competent Higher Tier response, but requiring further analysis and explanation for an improved result.

Christina Rossetti was born in 1830 and was brought up in a family of artists and writers. Christina and her sister were devout Christians. She refused to marry both of the men she loved because one was a Catholic and the other a non-Christian. She struggled against ill health for much of her life but her poetry reveals a belief in strong women and sympathy for those who 'fell'. She died of cancer in 1894.

First impressions

When you first read Rossetti's poems you may think they are simple and perhaps old-fashioned, about nature and relationships, and they are mainly sonnets or ballads. When you look more closely you will find that they are full of symbolism and profound meanings about the world of nature, the world of human relationships, and the world of the spirit. Rossetti uses themes of love, of grief, of loss, of unfaithfulness and constancy; and ideas about the nature of the material versus the spiritual life. You will notice the women in her poems are strong and nature often represents the eternal.

Stretch your skills

Use the titles of all the poems. Join them with words of your own, in any order you wish, to make a poem that represents your first impressions of Rossetti's work.

Now make your new poem into an audio-visual representation. You could stick words and pictures onto a large sheet of paper, accompanied by suitable music. You could make it into a PowerPoint presentation, with pictures, narration, and music or sound effects. You could ask someone to film you reading it, with introductory music and/or pictures.

Finish by asking other students what they think your impressions of the poems are.

ACTIVITY I

Work with a partner and write the following about the Rossetti poems that appear in your Anthology:

- what the title of each poem suggests
- what you expect each poem to be about.

Choose one poem and listen to a reading of it. Note down what else you learn about it.

Now create a visual representation of your chosen poem as a picture or a collage.

Imagery

Rossetti's images tend to be symbolic. She writes quite often about sexual relations or spiritual life in terms of fruit and flowers. Much of her imagery is taken from the natural world or from medieval ballads and paintings. She uses personification to express interactions between humans and nature and she can make striking contrasts as in 'I sit and howl in dust, / You sit in gold and sing'. Rossetti's use of metaphor provides phrases that inspire horror ('He feeds upon her face'), and joy ('A hovering melody of birds'), but often it has connotations of more profound ideas.

ACTIVITY 2

Work with a small group and choose one poem that you think contains striking imagery. Borrow some percussion instruments from the music department and use them to make sounds that express these images. Practise a reading of the poem with this accompaniment and perform it for the rest of the class. Ask them to guess why you chose the sounds.

Stretch your skills

Work with a partner and use a copy of the poem 'On the Wing'. Highlight all the images. Draw a storyboard outline that will fit all the images. In each square put a picture to represent the images, in order as they appear in the poem. There is an example below.

'We stood together in an open field'	'Above our heads two swift-winged pigeons wheeled'		

Discuss what you think the images represent. What might the hawk and the doves symbolize? Is there a sexual meaning to the poem? Make an image board for a poem of your choice.

Language

The language Rossetti uses in her poems is deceptively simple. It nearly always has a more profound meaning. Her techniques include sound patterning, and the use of repetition, like the adjective 'pale' in 'Maude Clare'. She uses conversation in several of the ballad poems and most of the texts include the first person pronoun, which involves the reader in her narrator's feelings. Her language is metaphorical and symbolic, like the blossoms in 'An Apple-Gathering' or 'the silent land' of 'Remember'. She also uses the different connotations of words to point meaning, like 'is' and 'was' in 'In an Artist's Studio'.

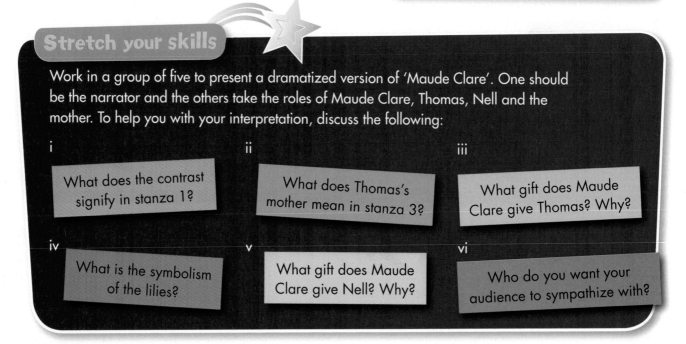

ACTIVITY 3

a Work with a partner and use a copy of the poem 'Cousin Kate'. Use different colours to highlight the following:

- examples of repetition
- examples of contrast
- examples of metaphor
- an example of an oxymoron.

b Write four short paragraphs explaining the effects of each of them.

c Write a letter as the narrator, telling the events of the poem to a friend.

Stretch your skills

Work in a group of five to present a dramatized version of 'Maude Clare'. One should be the narrator and the others take the roles of Maude Clare, Thomas, Nell and the mother. To help you with your interpretation, discuss the following:

i What does the contrast signify in stanza 1?

ii What does Thomas's mother mean in stanza 3?

iii What gift does Maude Clare give Thomas? Why?

iv What is the symbolism of the lilies?

v What gift does Maude Clare give Nell? Why?

vi Who do you want your audience to sympathize with?

Structure

Many of Rossetti's poems that appear in the Anthology are either sonnets or ballads. This gives them a traditional form and metre, although she sometimes uses half-rhymes which break the pattern slightly, like 'dim / dream' ('In an Artist's Studio') or she changes the rhythm of a line as in stanza 15 of 'In the Willow Shade'. Her poems tend to follow a narrative, like 'Cousin Kate', or create a situation which needs resolving, as in 'Shut Out', or follow a specific argument, as in 'The World'. Often the poems end without a resolution, with the narrator left in a kind of emotional or spiritual wilderness.

ACTIVITY 4

Work with a partner and draw a grid like the one below to include all the poems.

Poem title	Rhyme scheme	Rhythm	Form
The Key-Note	Changes between stanzas		
Spring Quiet			Five quatrains + final five-line stanza
A Dumb Friend		3 lines of iambic pentameter + one with three stresses	

Discuss how the structure of each poem helps its meaning.

Stretch your skills

a Copy the **sonnets** from the collection and put them side by side. Work with a partner to do the following:
- write which form each of the sonnets takes
- highlight the turning point in each of them
- annotate the rhyme scheme in each one and note similarities and differences
- summarize the 'argument' of each one, before and after the turning point.

b Write two or three short paragraphs about how the structure helps to bring out the meaning of the poems.

c Use no more than three sentences to explain why Rossetti has chosen the sonnet form.

Comparison

Rossetti's poems have strong feelings and situations that many readers will be able to relate to, as in 'No, Thank You, John', where she is trying to give the brush-off to a persistent suitor. In other poems she is struggling with her own conscience and beliefs, as in 'Shut Out' and 'The World'. Her use of symbolic nature, in fruit, flowers, trees and birds, can also be a point of comparison. The way Rossetti uses the connotations of words to give deeper meanings to her poems, like her use of 'shadow' in 'In the Willow Shade' also creates interesting comparisons.

ACTIVITY 5

Look at the poems 'Maude Clare' and 'Cousin Kate'. Use a Venn diagram like the one below to show points of similarity and difference.

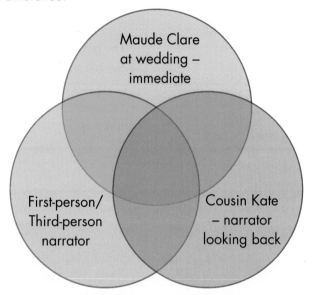

Maude Clare at wedding – immediate

First-person/ Third-person narrator

Cousin Kate – narrator looking back

Where the circles overlap you should include points of similarity; for example, both were victims of a great lord.

ACTIVITY 6

Compare the poems 'A Dumb Friend' and 'In the Willow Shade'. Think about the following:

- Which of these might represent 'the tree of life'?
- Why are there phrases like 'overshadowing', and 'Betwixt me and the sun' in poem 2?
- How are the trees similar and how are they different?

Write a paragraph comparing the poems.

Personal response

Rossetti has previously been dismissed by literary critics who felt her poems were too personal. Latterly, she has been reassessed by feminist critics who find her fierce independence and compassion for 'fallen women' (outcasts in her time) appealing. Her strong religious beliefs may find less sympathy but everyone can understand the struggle between what we want to do and what is our duty. You may enjoy her characters or her symbolism or the way she uses subtle shades of meaning in her language. It may be the traditional forms or the rhythms of her poems you like.

ACTIVITY 7

Imagine you have been asked to give a talk on your choice of Rossetti's poems from the Anthology. Put together a short talk, explaining what the poem is about and how effectively the poet conveys her ideas. You could use visual aids like spider diagrams, pictures and quotations in speech bubbles for the interactive white board to illustrate your talk.

ROSSETTI: SAMPLE TASKS

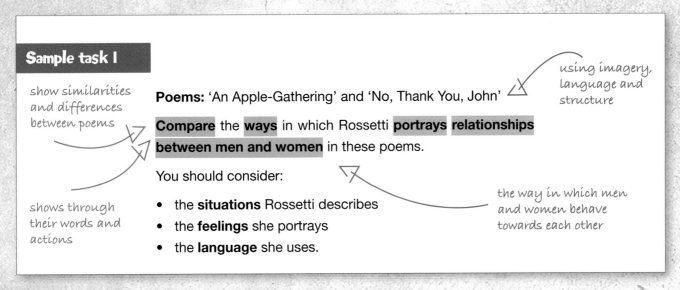

Sample task I

show similarities and differences between poems

Poems: 'An Apple-Gathering' and 'No, Thank You, John'

using imagery, language and structure

Compare the **ways** in which Rossetti **portrays relationships between men and women** in these poems.

You should consider:

- the **situations** Rossetti describes
- the **feelings** she portrays
- the **language** she uses.

shows through their words and actions

the way in which men and women behave towards each other

1. You could add further boxes with short quotations to this spider diagram:

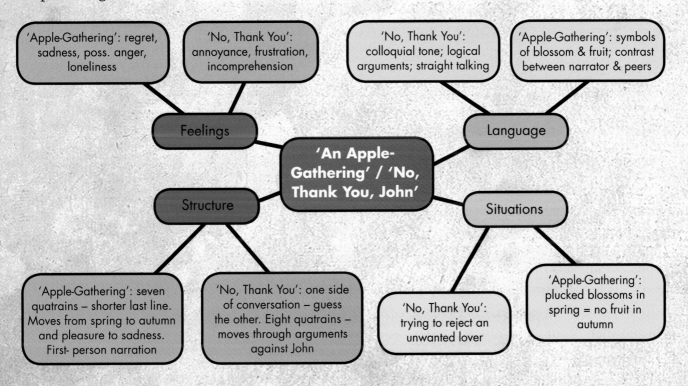

'Apple-Gathering': regret, sadness, poss. anger, loneliness

'No, Thank You': annoyance, frustration, incomprehension

'No, Thank You': colloquial tone; logical arguments; straight talking

'Apple-Gathering': symbols of blossom & fruit; contrast between narrator & peers

Feelings

Language

'An Apple-Gathering' / 'No, Thank You, John'

Structure

Situations

'Apple-Gathering': seven quatrains – shorter last line. Moves from spring to autumn and pleasure to sadness. First- person narration

'No, Thank You': one side of conversation – guess the other. Eight quatrains – moves through arguments against John

'No, Thank You': trying to reject an unwanted lover

'Apple-Gathering': plucked blossoms in spring = no fruit in autumn

2. Plan your answer based on parts of the question – relationships between men and women; how the reader is made aware of situation, feelings and language in each poem and how these are similar and different. Make sure you select appropriate quotations and embed them in your answer as evidence. An example of a plan is shown on the next page.

Opening

- situation noting circumstances of speakers

Development

- look at structure of 'An Apple-Gathering' – show how it brings out relationship
- comment on feelings as shown in language (including imagery) – with regard to relationships

Comparison

- look at structure of 'No, Thank You, John' and what it shows of relationships

- compare/contrast with 'An Apple-Gathering'
- comment on feelings as shown in language (including imagery) – relate to relationships and compare/contrast with 'An Apple-Gathering'

Conclusion

- difference made to relationships by situation.

Sample task 2

show similarities and differences between poems

using imagery, language and structure

Poems: 'In the Willow Shade' and 'Spring Quiet'

Compare the **ways** in which Rossetti **portrays** her **relationship with nature** in these poems.

You should consider:

- the **situations** Rossetti describes
- the **feelings** she portrays
- the **language** she uses.

shows through their words and actions

the poet's presentation of and emotional response to nature

Student response – Sample task 1

brief and concise overview of poems

In the poem 'An Apple-Gathering', Christina Rossetti shows a young girl who has been rejected by a man and has to watch him with another girl from the same village. In the poem 'No, Thank You, John', a girl is being pestered by a young man who wants to be her lover and won't take 'no' for an answer. She puts forward a number of arguments and then offers him friendship but not love.

summing up of differences in situation

The two girls are in opposite situations, as one has offered love and then been cast off, and the other has been offered love, but won't accept it.

Student response – Sample task I continued

understanding of metaphor →

In 'An Apple-Gathering' Rossetti writes about the relationship in terms of flowers and fruit. Apples were supposedly the fruit that Eve used to tempt Adam in the Garden of Eden and so they are symbolic of sinfulness and the expulsion of human beings from Paradise. The poem begins with a brief description of how 'I plucked pink blossoms from mine apple tree' and the narrator wore them 'in my hair' presumably to attract the young man. She sacrificed the chance of apples later in order to have what she wanted then. This may be a euphemism for giving herself to the man before they were married as she says they used to go 'Laughing and listening in this very lane'.

use of biblical allusion shows perception →

understanding of symbolic images →

← *fluently embedded quotations*

← *useful quotation that would have benefited from further explanation*

Unlike the narrator of 'An Apple-Gathering', the speaker in 'No, Thank You, John' is very firm in refusing his love despite the fact that he 'will...teaze me day by day'. She finds it annoying that he haunts her like 'an hour-old ghost' when she has made her feelings plain. Instead of watching sadly as the man goes with another girl, the narrator here encourages John, not in flattering terms, with 'I dare say Meg or Moll would take / Pity upon you'. The language used in the first poem is metaphorical and euphemistic, while the second is direct and colloquial.

well-chosen quotation – though needed evaluating →

understanding of technical terms →

← *explicit point of contrast in situation and feeling*

EXAMINER'S COMMENTS OCR

- The student shows a good grasp of metaphor and of technical terms in their answer, as well as a clear understanding of the points of contrast between the two poems.
- The answer is perceptive, with clear support from both poems.
- This is a good Higher Tier response, but further analysis and explanation would produce a better result.

Sonnets

Although he is widely considered the greatest writer in the English language, relatively little is known about Shakespeare's life. Born in Stratford in 1654, he married Anne Hathaway at 18, after she became pregnant. He went to London, leaving his wife and three children behind, to seek his fortune. He was lucky to get some rich backers for his poetry. He also worked in a theatre and learned how to write plays. He wrote 37 plays, 154 sonnets and some long poems. He died in Stratford in 1616.

First impressions

These sonnets are all love poems. Some appear to address a man and some a woman. There has been much debate surrounding Shakespeare's sexuality; it is not known for sure whether he was bisexual. The young man he writes about was probably a patron. The woman could have been a mistress.

The sonnets may seem difficult to understand at first. They use logical arguments and word play. Another barrier can be Shakespeare's language. English has changed a lot since these poems were written. Words can die out or change their meanings over time. In Sonnet 43 'wink' means to sleep, like 'forty winks'.

ACTIVITY I

In the Controlled Assessment, you will be asked to compare two sonnets which have a shared theme. Read through all the sonnets and create a chart of themes they address:

Sonnet 2	ageing, parenthood
Sonnet 3	
Sonnet 15	
Sonnet 18	beauty, nature, immortality, writing poetry

This will give you:

- a quick overview of all the poems
- an idea of the possible combinations you might be set
- an indication of Shakespeare's preoccupations.

Choose one of the sonnets at random, and read it aloud several times. Then write a version of it in modern prose. Example for Sonnet 2:

When you're forty and your face is wrinkled and your good looks gone, and people ask you what happened to your face, it won't really help to say you ruined it with partying. But if you can point to your son and say he's got your good looks now, that will make you feel a lot better about ageing. By looking at him you will feel young again, because he would be like you once were.

Imagery

Personification was a popular technique in Shakespeare's time, so figures like Death (the Reaper), Time and Love are often turned into people. Another convention is love as a sickness, which is treated by physic (medicine). Shakespeare is also fond of imagery drawn from nature. In Sonnet 73, Shakespeare calls trees 'Bare ruined choirs', meaning choir stalls. Trees are now empty of birds, just like the choir stalls of ruined abbeys are abandoned by the singers and left exposed to the open air. Sometimes the imagery is densely packed like this. The best way to appreciate it is to explore connections.

ACTIVITY 2

Look at Sonnet 116 on page 99 of your Anthology. Shakespeare finds imagery to express the permanence of love.

Fill in the blanks:

Quotation	Explanation	Evaluation
	Love cannot be rubbed out with an eraser	This is effective because only mistakes are rubbed out. True love is written in indelible ink, it cannot be erased no matter what.
It is the star to every wandering barque	Ships were guided by the stars in Shakespeare's time because there was no other way.	
Love's not Time's fool, though rosy lips and cheeks/ Within his bending sickle's compass come		

Stretch your skills

Choose any sonnet and create a PowerPoint presentation or a poster of the words combined with some appropriate pictures to illustrate the imagery. Ask your teacher if you can show your work to the class, or print it out and ask for it to be displayed.

Language

There are several things you might notice:

- all the sonnets are addressed to someone, using the second person
- 'thou', 'thee' and 'thy' are used because in Shakespeare's time this was how people addressed family and close friends
- some of the language sounds old and meanings have changed
- 'th' endings are 's' in modern English, e.g. doth = does; fadeth = fades, etc.
- there may be repetition and word play
- the rhymes hold the sonnet together and link ideas
- each line has a strong pattern of iambics (unstressed and stressed syllables in pairs).

ACTIVITY 3

Choose two sonnets and read through them, highlighting language that seems difficult to you. Discuss your examples with a partner and, using a dictionary if necessary, try to untangle the language until you feel more confident.

Stretch your skills

Most of the adjectives have been removed from this sonnet. Imagine you are writing it and fill them in. Then compare your version with Shakespeare's. Why do you think he has made these choices and what do the adjectives add to the poem?

Since brass, nor stone, nor earth, nor _____ sea,
But _____ mortality o'ersways their power,
How with this rage shall beauty hold a plea,
Whose action is no stronger than a flower?
O how shall summer's _____ breath hold out
Against the _____ siege of _____ days,
When rocks _____ are not so _____,
Nor gates of steel so _____, but time decays?
O fearful meditation; where, alack,
Shall Time's _____ jewel from Time's chest lie hid?
Or what _____ hand can hold his _____ foot back,
Or who his spoil of beauty can forbid?
   O none, unless this miracle have might,
   That in _____ ink my love may still shine _____.

Structure

Consider how Shakespeare fits his argument to the sonnet form by looking at the order of ideas. For example, Sonnet 3 (page 94) aims to persuade a young man to have children by listing reasons, by flattery and by giving examples. At the start of the poem Shakespeare refers to a mirror in which the young man is looking. By line 9, the mirror has become metaphorical: the young man is the mirror image of his mother, and a child would in turn mirror him. The mirror is a structural device: it holds the poem together.

ACTIVITY 4

Sonnets usually have a 'turn' in which the argument is reversed. Take the first two lines and the last two lines of one of these sonnets and try to predict how Shakespeare arrives at the change. Then check out the whole sonnet and see if you are correct. Try this out on 18, 19, 73, and 130, as they all have clear turns.

Stretch your skills

a Not all the sonnets in this selection have turns. Many use the final couplet as a conclusion. Read through all the sonnets. Annotate according to how Shakespeare uses the couplet.

b Often the imagery holds the sonnet together, for example, Sonnet 18 draws on summer throughout. Read all the sonnets and highlight extended imagery.

c Sometimes the rhyme schemes help to divide the argument into sections. Sonnet 73 is an obvious example. Study 73 to get the idea; read more to find further examples.

d Using a printed copy, slice up a sonnet into pairs of lines. Try to work out the correct order.

Comparison

For your Controlled Assessment, you will be asked to compare any two of these sonnets, using a thematic link. It is a good idea to look for links as you study them, as there is only a limited pool of questions you can be given, based on the sonnets selected for you from the 154 Shakespeare wrote. For example, the first two share the idea that having children is a way to make oneself immortal. The sonnets have smaller links too, like shared imagery, or shared purpose. It is also essential to compare how the sonnet form is employed.

ACTIVITY 5

Thematic Map

Read through the sonnets and create a mind map of the different themes and the sonnets that relate to them:

Themes — Immortality through poetry — 15 / 18

Continue this mindmap until you have linked all the sonnets together.

Choose pairs of sonnets from your mindmap. List ways in which they differ and/or are similar.

For example:

Sonnet 15 and 18

Both use imagery from nature, but 15 uses plants and 18 uses a season.
15 personifies Time, 18 Death.

Personal response

Personal response is where you get your chance to say why you enjoy certain sonnets more than others. It might include personal reasons, such as Sonnet 73 might make you think of your grandfather, or you might enjoy the romance of 18, or the wit of 130. You could also write about an image you find particularly effective. You might have found a particular sonnet difficult to start with and have grown to love it from close reading, feeling satisfied that you can now grasp it.

A personal response should never be 'it's boring' because that shows you haven't taken the trouble to listen to it properly.

Stretch your skills

Using your lists from the last exercise, make a comparison chart, including quotations, to practise the skills you will need in the assignment.

You should only allow yourself ten minutes for this exercise, so use note form and work against the clock. This is all the time you can allow yourself before you start writing your response when doing the assignment for real.

However tempting it may be to just dive in, it is not a good idea. Some people, after much practice, can plan in their minds. But writing down a quick plan helps, so long as you make sure you follow it!

ACTIVITY 6

Re-read all the sonnets, and rate them, giving up to 10 stars for the ones you prefer. You must give at least one star. Then choose your five most highly rated and explain your rating, either to a partner, the whole class, or in a mini-review.

Imagine Shakespeare's sonnets being performed on a CD. Review it for a music magazine.

SHAKESPEARE: SAMPLE TASKS

Love and beauty are two different ideas. You should write about them both and link them.

Task

Compare the **ways** in which Shakespeare **portrays love and beauty** in Sonnet 18 and Sonnet 116.

You should consider:

- the **situations** Shakespeare describes
- the **feelings** he portrays
- the **language** he uses.

Note the word 'should'. This means that you must follow the bullet points.

Use the bullet points to structure your answer. They give you your topic paragraphs.

Read the question and highlight the key words

Compare the ways in which Shakespeare portrays love and beauty in Sonnet 18 and Sonnet 116.

Re-read the sonnets.
Use the bullet points to structure a plan.
Annotation will also form part of your planning.

The situations Shakespeare describes
18, 116
The feelings he portrays
18, 116
The language he uses
18, 116

You can address the third bullet point all the way through your assignment

Start your assignment by giving an overview of your ideas. Make points, not predictions.

Tips for writing a brilliant assignment

1. Remember, the bullet points are there to guide you but are not the question.

2. All your points must refer to the question, in this case how **love** and **beauty** are portrayed.

3. Refer only to the specified sonnets.

4. Discuss the poems together, but it helps if you always lead with the one that is listed first in the question.

5. To help your teacher mark your assignment, keep it logical. Deal with the first bullet point first, etc.

6. Use comparison words such as: *on the other hand, whereas, similar, in contrast, different, linked by, both.*

7. Keep quotations brief. Even a single well-chosen word can back your point up perfectly.

8. Be brave and think for yourself. The question will stimulate you into new insights.

9. Avoid repeating yourself. Your work will not be given extra marks for being unnecessarily lengthy.

10. Check off your plan as you go by ticking things you have done.

11. Write a punchy conclusion, including some personal response, such as which sonnet you felt portrayed love and beauty most effectively.

Sample task 2

Notice the question begins 'compare the ways'. The wording might vary, but the task stays the same.

Task

Compare the **ways** in which Shakespeare **portrays** the **passage of time** and its **effects** in Sonnet 2 and Sonnet 3.

You should consider:

- the **situations** Shakespeare describes
- the **feelings** he portrays
- the **language** he uses.

The bullet points are the same. These are the things you are given marks for.

The last bullet point includes structure and imagery as well as language.

Student response – Sample task I (opening paragraphs)

Sonnets 18 and 116 share similar ideas about love and beauty. In 18, Shakespeare flatters a woman by saying she is more beautiful than a summer's day. He loves her so much he is writing the poem just to make her immortal. However, he seems to love her for her beauty alone as he does not write anything about her personality.

Sonnet 116, on the other hand, talks about how nothing can alter true love, even if the woman loses her beauty over time. Although the first poem is flattery, the second is more like true love.

The situations are the same in both poems as Shakespeare is talking to a woman, telling her how beautiful she is. But the second one is more about love than 18, which is more about him loving his own writing, as in the turn he says:

So long as men can breathe or eyes can see,

So long lives this, and this gives life to thee.

this punchy sentence sums up the comparisons discovered in the opening paragraph

the wording of the topic sentence signals the first bullet point is being addressed

the first sentence gets straight into comparing and addresses the question

notice the long quotation is set out exactly as in the poem; shorter ones are embedded

He says his writing is 'eternal' and is making her beauty eternal. But there is no love declared for the pretty girl; the poem could be addressed to any good-looking woman. The second poem is defining love, and might not even be talking to anyone in particular. Instead of being all about beauty, it says that true love is a 'marriage of true minds', that personality matters more than beauty where love is concerned.

Shakespeare's feelings in 18 are appreciation of the girl's perfection: 'Thou art more lovely' than a 'summer's day', and pride in his own writing, whereas in 116, he is a man in ardent love, and promising his love will outlast 'rosy lips and cheeks'.

He uses some wonderful language in 116. He says true love is 'the star to every wandering barque', which is very apt as ships would have got lost without the stars to navigate by. Stars are associated with love, fate and romance. 18 also uses sky imagery, but about the sun, calling it 'the eye of heaven', so this poem seems less private because it is set in the daytime.

the student neatly contrasts the two sonnets

This essay would continue by looking into more detail about the language, as an overview has now been given.

EXAMINER'S COMMENTS OCR

- This is a focused and well-written response in the Higher Tier range.
- The student shows clear understanding of the contrasts between the two poems and offers their own impressions and responses to the writing, supporting these interpretations with apt quotations from the text.

Section 3

Contemporary Poets

HOW TO APPROACH THE EXAM (FOR ENGLISH LITERATURE)

How will I be assessed?

This unit is tested by an exam. In the Contemporary Poetry section, you will need to answer **one** question. The question can be **either**

- on one of the six set contemporary poets

or

- on a single unseen poem (that you have not previously studied).

Here are the six set poets, **one** of whom you might choose to study:

- Simon Armitage
- Gillian Clarke
- Wendy Cope
- Carol Ann Duffy
- Seamus Heaney
- Benjamin Zephaniah.

What will the questions be like?

If you choose to answer a question on a **set poet**, you will have a choice of three questions. The first question will be on a poem printed on the question paper. The second and third questions will ask you to comment on, criticize and analyse **one** poem from a choice of two poems by the poet you have studied.

If you choose to answer a question on an **unseen poem**, the poem will be printed on the question paper and you will be asked to comment on, criticize and analyse it. This poem will **not** appear in your *Reflections* Anthology.

What will I be assessed on?

In the Unit 4 exam, you will be tested on the Assessment Objectives listed below.

- **AO1: Respond to the texts critically and imaginatively; select and evaluate relevant textual detail to illustrate and support interpretations.**

  This means that you need to show how you understand and interpret the text, using quotations to explain your ideas and responses.

- **AO2: Explain how language, structure and form contribute to writers' presentation of ideas, themes and settings.**

  This means that you need to show an overall understanding of the language features, structure and form that the writer has used and be able to explain the effects these produce on the reader.

As in all the units for English Literature, the quality of your 'written communication' will be assessed. This means that you need to:

- ensure your text is legible, and that spelling, punctuation and grammar are accurate so that the meaning is clear
- present information in a form that suits its purpose
- use a suitable structure and style of writing.

Simon Armitage

The popular, award-winning Yorkshire poet Simon Armitage was born in 1963. After studying Geography at university, he worked as a probation officer. His poetry is often distinguished by his choice of gritty, dramatic subjects and his bold, vivid use of language. His poetry collections include *Kid*, *The Dead Sea Poems* and *Book of Matches* (which gained its title as each poem should take no longer to read than the burning of a match).

First impressions

Armitage's poetry is striking both in how it appears on the page and how it sounds when read aloud. Looking through his poems in your Anthology, you will notice that the poems vary in length and layout. Some have evocative titles like 'Gooseberry Season', while others take the first line of the poem as their title or one, even more simply, is called 'Poem'. Many are written in the first person, yet, in some cases, it is clear that the speaker is not Armitage himself. Some of the poems use 'slang', while others are more lyrical.

Stretch your skills

'About His Person' sums up a person's life by the few items found 'about his person' upon his death. It could be said that the reader is placed in the role of a 'detective' who is piecing together the character's biography from this meagre evidence. Armitage skilfully suggests the sadness and despair of the man's life.

Try writing your own 'About His (or Her) Person' poem. Choose a character from history or fiction and make a list of what clues would remain about his or her life after death. Now shape this evidence into your poem.

ACTIVITY I

Read the poems 'About His Person' (page 105) and 'Gooseberry Season' (page 107) and compare your first impressions using the grid below:

	'About His Person'	'Gooseberry Season'
How does the poem look on the page?		
What is the poem about?		
Are there any recurring sounds or patterns?		
What is the mood or tone of the poem?		
Do you like this poem?		

With a partner, read the poem 'Alaska' (page 106) silently and then aloud.
Next complete the following spider diagram with your ideas about this poem.

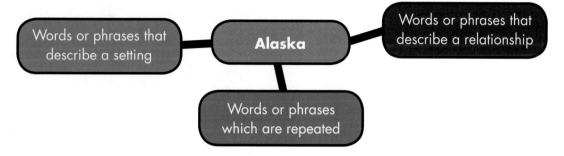

Words or phrases that describe a setting — **Alaska** — Words or phrases that describe a relationship — Words or phrases which are repeated

Now write a paragraph describing your first impressions of this poem.

Imagery

Simon Armitage is known for his portrayals of relationships, settings (particularly the North), journeys, social class, nature and conflict. To explore these ideas he uses a range of imagery, such as similes and metaphors. Some metaphors are used very bluntly, such as 'Anchor. Kite.' to depict the relationship between a mother and son, while others, like the harebell in 'In Our Tenth Year' (page 109) are extended; in this case, to describe a couple's close relationship. When reading the poems, make sure that you note the effect the imagery has on you.

ACTIVITY 3

Read the similes below. Identify in which poem you will find the simile and what it suggests to you.

Simile	Poem	What it suggests to you
'dragged him like a mattress'		
'fist dithered like a compass needle'		
'like the practice scales of a Grade 1 cornet lesson'		
'deliver on the run like parachute drops'		
'like a big kodiak bear'		

ACTIVITY 4

In 'To Poverty' (page 116) poverty is **personified** as a constant presence in the speaker's life. Read the quotations in the speech bubbles below and then write your impression of poverty.

'I've tried too long to see the back of you.'

'How have you hurt me....'

'I'd rather keep you in the corner of my eye...'

In his poems, Armitage makes many allusions to poetry and other forms of literature and entertainment. For example, 'To Poverty' is inspired by a poem by a Lancashire poet, Samuel Laycock (1826–1893,) and contains references to other poets such as Elizabeth Barrett Browning (who wrote 'How do I love thee? Let me count the ways') and Robert Frost. As you read the poems, note and research any references you can find to the following:

- other poets or their poems
- other forms of media, such as films or comic books.

Language

Simon Armitage's poetry uses language in a rich and sometimes surprising way. His poems frequently employ alliteration, rhyme (including near or 'half' rhymes), lists of three and connotation. He also uses slang or colloquial language, which give many of his poems a very contemporary and conversational tone. For example, in 'Kid', Armitage mimics both the tone and diction of British tabloid newspapers and American comic books. In 'My father thought it bloody queer', Armitage recreates the dialogue between a father and son, including the blunt insults.

ACTIVITY 5

Look at the speech bubbles opposite, which contain phrases spoken by characters in Armitage's poems. Identify the character and poem. Next, write down what you learn about these characters by the language they use.

'The truth... was blowin' in the wind'

'You should've had it through your nose instead.'

'You upped and went. Big deal!'

SECTION 3

ACTIVITY 6

Look at the quotations below from the poem 'Kid' (page 110) and analyse what language techniques Armitage is using and their effects on the reader.

Quotation	Language technique(s)	Effect on reader
'Batman, big shot'	Colloquial language and alliteration	
'ditched me'		
'let the cat out on that caper'		
'Holy robin-redbreast-nest-egg-shocker!'		
'taller, harder, stronger, older'		

Structure

Simon Armitage explores a range of structures and forms in his poetry. 'Poem' is a **sonnet**, ending with a rhyming couplet, which sums up the admirable and less admirable aspects of a man's life. 'Kid' and 'Hitcher' are both **dramatic monologues** in which Armitage creates characters facing decisive moments. 'The Convergence of the Twain' is a series of **tercets** (three lines), numbered with roman numerals, in reference to the poem of the same name by Thomas Hardy (page 57). When reading the poems, always consider the impact the structure and form have on the reader.

ACTIVITY 7

Use the chart below to compare the structure of 'Poem' (page 113) and 'Wintering Out' (page 118).

Structure/Form	'Poem'	'Wintering Out'
Rhyming pattern (if any)		
Number of stanzas		
Lines in each stanza		
Regular rhythm/metre		
Order in which events of poem are told		

Then write a paragraph comparing the structure and form of these two poems and say which you prefer.

ACTIVITY 8

Sonnets are a powerful form for exploring intense emotion in relatively few lines. Which of Armitage's poems would you classify as being sonnets, and how would you compare them to the other sonnets in this Anthology?

Stretch your skills

Simon Armitage has said:

'It's the job of art to create or even invent significance.'

Read his poem 'The Convergence of the Twain' (page 114), inspired by the attack on the World Trade Centre and Thomas Hardy's poem (page 57) in response to the sinking of the Titanic. In both cases, the poets are writing about a major event and giving it significance. Choose a major current event that interests you and write your own poem copying the form of 'The Convergence of the Twain.'

Personal response

As you read the poetry of Simon Armitage you may experience different personal responses. You may be shocked by the violence of 'Hitcher' or 'Gooseberry Season' or feel sympathy for the speaker in 'To Poverty.' Many readers identify with his portrayals of relationships between parents and children in poems like 'Mother, any distance...' or 'My father thought it...', or between couples in 'In Our Tenth Year.' Others find poems like 'Kid' playful and funny. Highlight any words or phrases which you find particularly striking and explain their effect.

ACTIVITY 9

Use the chart below to explore your response to Armitage's portrayal of family relationships.

Relationship	Quotation	Personal response
Father	'me and the old man/made a good team'	
Husband	'And once, for laughing, punched her in the face'	
Mother	'your fingertips still pinch/the last one-hundredth of an inch'	
Mother-in-law	'your mother/having one of her moments....'	

ACTIVITY 10

Use the spider diagram opposite to note your personal responses to Armitage's depiction of violence.

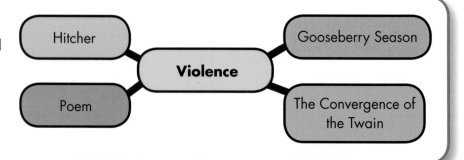

ARMITAGE: SAMPLE TASKS

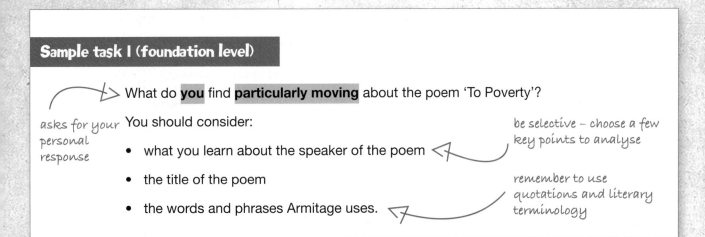

Sample task I (foundation level)

What do **you** find **particularly moving** about the poem 'To Poverty'?

asks for your personal response

You should consider:

- what you learn about the speaker of the poem

- the title of the poem

- the words and phrases Armitage uses.

be selective – choose a few key points to analyse

remember to use quotations and literary terminology

Some students find it useful to make a spider diagram to develop their ideas. For this question, your spider diagram might look something like this:

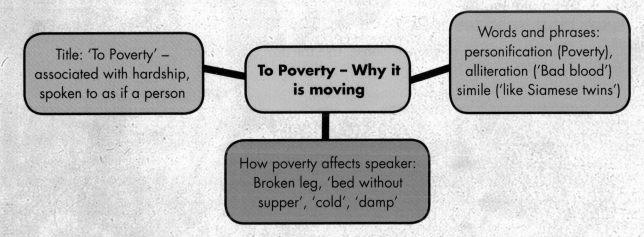

Title: 'To Poverty' – associated with hardship, spoken to as if a person

To Poverty – Why it is moving

Words and phrases: personification (Poverty), alliteration ('Bad blood') simile ('like Siamese twins')

How poverty affects speaker: Broken leg, 'bed without supper', 'cold', 'damp'

You are being asked to analyse the poem rather than simply retell what it is about. Look at the two sample responses below and decide which you think is better and why.

Response I

There are a lot of techniques in the poem 'To Poverty.' Armitage uses similes and imagery which makes it very sad. The poem is about someone who is poor and we learn what a bad time he has had, such as breaking his legs.

Response 2

Through the use of similes, such as 'like sidekicks' and 'like Siamese twins,' Armitage emphasizes how the speaker cannot escape from poverty; it is permanently attached to him. However, unlike Siamese twins who might be joined at the 'hip', the speaker is joined to poverty at the 'pocket', emphasizing his lack of money. The sound 's' is repeated in the first stanza: 'shadow', 'silhouette' and 'shape'. The hissing 's' sound and these ominous words suggests the speaker's sad and frightening situation.

Structuring your response

Take a few minutes to structure your response. Use the flow chart below to help you answer the question above.

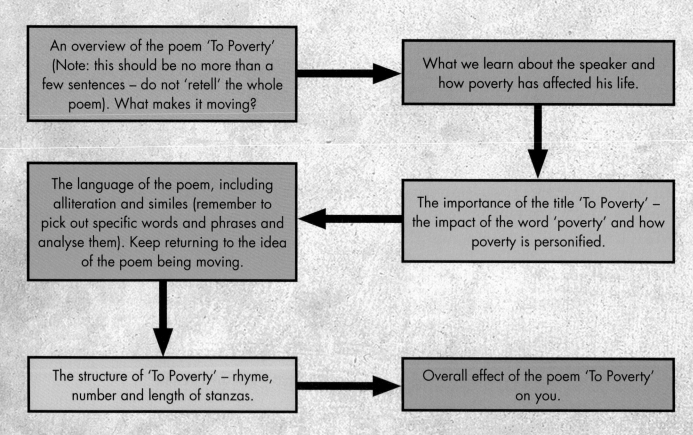

An overview of the poem 'To Poverty' (Note: this should be no more than a few sentences – do not 'retell' the whole poem). What makes it moving?

→

What we learn about the speaker and how poverty has affected his life.

The importance of the title 'To Poverty' – the impact of the word 'poverty' and how poverty is personified.

The language of the poem, including alliteration and similes (remember to pick out specific words and phrases and analyse them). Keep returning to the idea of the poem being moving.

The structure of 'To Poverty' – rhyme, number and length of stanzas.

→

Overall effect of the poem 'To Poverty' on you.

Sample task 2 (foundation level)

What do you think is especially **frightening and sinister** about **EITHER** 'Poem' **OR** 'Gooseberry Season'?

threatening or suggesting evil or harm

make a choice between the poems – don't write about both

Remember to refer closely to the words and phrases Armitage uses in your chosen poem.

select key words and phrases to write about

Student response – Sample task I (foundation level)

immediately addresses the question

In the poem, 'To Poverty,' Simon Armitage creates a powerful and moving impression of how poverty has affected the life of the speaker. He portrays poverty as a constant presence in the life of the speaker, hurting him and leaving him hungry and in pain.

The speaker in the poem has known poverty 'for years' and has suffered greatly. It is particularly moving to learn in the fourth stanza that when he broke both legs, he could not afford to have them set. Armitage highlights the hopelessness of his situation by repeating 'wait', which is the only choice the poor have. He uses many words to show that poverty is always with him. Similes 'like Siamese twins', and 'like sidekicks' suggest that they cannot be separated and poverty has always been 'struck' with him.

internal quotation effectively used

effective analysis of how poet uses literary techniques

An unusual feature of the poem is that poverty is personified. The title of the poem, 'To Poverty', informs us that poverty is both the subject of the poem and the 'person' to whom the poem is addressed. The use of personification makes poverty a powerful presence in the poem, someone who can 'shadow' the speaker. This is particularly moving because poverty becomes a real and haunting figure in the life of the speaker.

good analysis, thoughtfully explained

Armitage's choice of particular words and phrases highlights the effects of poverty. Poverty is shown as a mysterious and frightening figure, emphasized by the repetition of words beginning with 's': 'shadow', 'shape', 'silhouette'. Alliteration, such as the phrase 'Bad blood' reinforces the harmful effect of poverty, suggesting both illness and anger. Alliteration is also used to highlight the physical discomfort of poverty such as hunger, 'bread without butter'. He substitutes the word 'hurt' for the word 'love' to show how damaging poverty is.

In the final stanza of the poem, the speaker's direct and positive approach to dealing with poverty is both moving and impressive. He repeats the phrase 'sit down' to show that he has not yet been conquered and will continue to face up to the challenges of being poor.

effective analysis of how poet uses literary techniques

EXAMINER'S COMMENTS OCR

RECOGNISING ACHIEVEMENT

- This is a good Foundation Tier response, as it shows clear appreciation of the poet's use of language and the effect of the literary effects chosen.
- Interpretations are well explained and supported with effective quotations from the poem.

Sample task 3 (higher level)

Look for aspects of the poems which are funny, playful, or interesting.

In what **ways** does Armitage make **EITHER** 'Kid' **OR** 'True North' so **amusing and entertaining**?

Remember to refer closely to the **language** Armitage uses in your chosen poem.

Choose the poem about which you can make the most points.

Remember to use literary terminology for the key words and phrases you analyse.

Both 'Kid' and 'True North' are amusing and entertaining poems, so either could be chosen to answer this question well. 'Kid' is clearly a humorous poem told from the point of view of Batman's sidekick, Robin. 'True North' is a more reflective, autobiographical account of returning home for Christmas after a term at university. Use the chart below and decide which poem you feel you could use most successfully for this question.

	'Kid'	'True North'
Amusing or entertaining topic	Robin 'comes of age' and puts Batman in his place	
Amusing or entertaining words or phrases		'toy snow-storm' 'ticker-tape welcome'
Interesting use of literary techniques such as similes, alliteration, metaphors		
Personal response: which poem most engages your interest?		

It is vital that you select and analyse appropriate evidence from your chosen poem. Look at the quotations below from these poems and explain how you could use them to show that these are amusing and entertaining poems:

'Holy robin-redbreast-nest-egg-shocker!'

'As the guests yawned their heads off'

'stewing over chicken giblets'

In order to get top marks, it is important to discuss the form and structure of your chosen poem.

- 'Kid' is written as one long stanza. How does this affect your enjoyment of this poem?
- 'True North' makes frequent use of enjambment. How does this contribute to your understanding of the poet's journey?
- Every line of 'Kid' ends with the sound 'er.' How does this add to the playfulness of the poem?

Sample task 4 (higher level)

In what **ways** does Armitage create a **memorably threatening atmosphere** in **EITHER** 'The Convergence of the Twin' **OR** 'Hitcher'?

Remember to refer closely to the **language** Armitage uses in your chosen poem.

How are the tone and mood of the poem created?

Look for powerful, menacing phrases and literary techniques.

Analyse specific words and phrases, using the correct terminology.

Student response – Sample task 3 (higher level)

effective opening paragraph; immediately indicating a grasp of the question

Simon Armitage's humorous poem 'Kid' uses a number of techniques such as alliteration, colloquial language and repetition to explore playfully Robin's resentment of Batman's previous power over him. Written as a dramatic monologue, it shows Robin forcefully rejecting his former mentor, Batman, and forging a new independent identity for himself. Although entertaining and comic, the poem also serves as an extended metaphor for any young person who outgrows someone who was 'like a father' or 'like an elder brother' to them.

demonstrating insight into deeper meaning of the poem

The poem begins with the surprising alliterative phrase 'Batman, big shot' alerting the reader both to the subject of the poem and Robin's disdainful attitude. Throughout the poem, Armitage uses colloquial language; for example, 'ditched' and 'sacked' to show how Batman has treated Robin. Armitage also imitates language from the Batman comics, such as 'Holy robin-readbreast' and from British tabloid newspapers, 'downtown on expenses in the motor'. This creates an amusing mix of verbal wordplay to entertain and surprise the reader.

clearly showing how poet's use of language has an effect on the reader

good explanation of how the poet has used literary techniques; showing their effect on the poem

One of the key elements of entertainment in this poem is the way Armitage challenges conventional perceptions of the

Student response – Sample task 3 (higher level) continued

character of Batman. This Batman is cruel to Robin, has an affair with a married woman, misuses his 'expenses' and is ultimately seen pathetically alone cooking an unappealing meal of 'chicken giblets'. This is very different from the heroic and mysterious Batman known to the reader through comic books and films. The alliterative phrase 'punching the palm of your hand' emphasizes his impotence.

good explanation of how the poet has used literary techniques; showing their effect on the poem

The poem is written as a single 24-line stanza, with the sound 'er' amusingly concluding each line. This makes the reader look forward to this series of rhymes and near-rhymes. The lack of separate stanzas gives the impression that this is a continuous 'rant' from Robin as he vents his fury, highlighting the comedy of the situation. In the course of this single stanza, Robin grows from rejected sidekick to someone who is 'taller, harder, stronger, older' (more repetitions of 'er'). He becomes the ultimate 'boy wonder', a term from his past which he reinvents to suggest something more dangerous and challenging.

useful comment on structure, showing how it works to shape the poem

EXAMINER'S COMMENTS OCR

- This is a sophisticated response to the poem, demonstrating both a strong understanding of structure and a perceptive analysis of the effects of the poets language choices.
- The answer is focused and well-structured, leading the reader through the argument well.
- This is a strong response within the Higher Tier range.

Gillian Clarke

Gillian Clarke was born in 1937 and has become one of the best-known Welsh poets of modern times. She has published a number of poetry collections, including some for children, and became the National Poet of Wales in 2008. She lives on an organic farm in Ceredigion, West Wales, and has founded a writers' centre as well as editing the 'Anglo-Welsh Review'. She also writes about her poetry online, to help students who are studying it.

First impressions

When you read Gillian Clarke's work you may be struck by the way she uses things that happen in her everyday life to make poems. Her poems are about Welsh rural life, about memories from her childhood and about time passing. She writes about the situation of women and about being a poet and a mother. Her poems are also shaped by Welsh legends and by fairy stories as well as how things that happen to one person or family can be related to universal human experience. Journeys take her through a human as well as a geographical landscape.

ACTIVITY I

a Make a list of the titles of Clarke's poems in the Anthology.

b Discuss with a partner what you think each poem might be about from its title.

c Group the titles under suitable headings such as 'nature', 'memories', 'journeys', 'time', etc.

d Compare your groupings with others. Discuss any similarities and differences and decide if you wish to make changes.

Choose one of Clarke's poems. Work with a partner and take turns to read it aloud.
Make a grid like the one below, using your own comments.

Poem Title

Rhythm and metre	What kind of rhythm? What does it suggest?	quotations to support your ideas
Sound patterns	Use of techniques. The effect of these.	quotations to support your ideas
Situation and feelings	What is the situation in the poem? What are the feelings presented?	quotations to support your ideas
Language and images	What do you notice about language use? What images catch your attention?	quotations to support your ideas

Imagery

Gillian Clarke's images are often striking; sometimes rich, as when she describes cream as 'standing gold' ('Anorexic') but sometimes spare and harsh like 'the bleached bone in the terminal ward' ('Baby-sitting'). She sees everyday things in a new way, as in 'The motorway straightens through the eyes of bridges' ('Coming Home') or captures a special moment through symbols, 'the daffodils are flame' ('Miracle on St David's Day'). Clarke can phrase an action to make us think in a different way, as in 'my mother gave a stranger's child her breath' ('Cold Knap Lake') or connect concrete things with abstract ideas of poetry and time, 'harvested apples and words and days' ('My Box').

ACTIVITY 2

Choose one poem and work with a partner. Read the poem aloud and underline the subject of the poem. Note any themes and ideas you can see in the poem, like nature, memory, time, childhood, the life of women, suffering, etc. Draw or find a picture that represents each of these themes, then make a visual collage that encapsulates the poem.

ACTIVITY 3

a Copy the poems 'Sunday' and 'The Angelus'. Work with a partner and highlight the images in both poems.
b Discuss why you think Clarke has chosen these images. What do they suggest about childhood and memory? How do they also link with the stories of childhood and children's observations?
c Write two paragraphs for each poem answering these questions.

Language

Gillian Clarke's language has been described as 'concrete', meaning it deals with solid things, as in 'the field lies bleeding' ('The Field-Mouse'). It is also economical, as a good poet's language should be, expressing profound things in a few words, like 'wolves howl into silent telephones' ('On the Train'). She uses contrast to show differences in lives and times, as in 'ill and penniless' / 'whisky gold in my glass' ('Marged'). Clarke also uses details to create a feeling, 'in its eyes / a sudden fall of snow' ('Hare in July') or 'a snuffly / Roseate, bubbling sleep' ('Baby-sitting'). Her language is musical in its sounds and rhythms.

ACTIVITY 6

Look at 'The Field-Mouse' (page 133). This links the damage done to creatures at harvest with the Bosnian war. Put your views about language into a spider diagram.

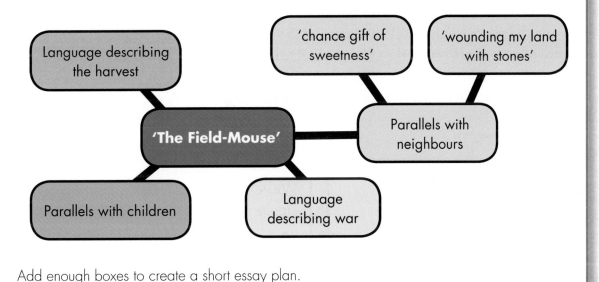

Add enough boxes to create a short essay plan.

Stretch your skills

Gillian Clarke makes language work on more than one level. Look at 'On the Train'. Complete the grid, using the phrases below.

Phrase	Literal meaning	Implied meaning
'the black box of my Walkman'	She has a personal stereo	The 'black box' is the recorder recovered from aircraft after a crash –associated with disaster.

'towards the blazing bone-ship.'

'phones ring in the rubble'

'Tonight I'll be home safe'

'wolves howl into silent telephones'

'Darling, I'm on the train.'

Re-write the poem as a text message to reassure a friend. What have you lost from the poem?

Structure

Gillian Clarke uses a range of structures and forms. These include the free-verse form of 'Baby-sitting', which echoes the reflective but almost fearful tone; the sonnet form of 'Marged', fitted to a historical/present time switch; the flowing iambic pentameter triplets of 'The Hare', which are at once a memorial and a celebration; and the skipping, changing metre of 'The Angelus', as it recalls the bells and rhythms of her convent- school youth. The poems work towards a resolution, a final thought or action, often with a turning point along the way.

ACTIVITY 7

Work with a partner and look at 'Baby-sitting' (page 123).

- Read it aloud, swapping over at the end of each **sentence**.
- What do you notice about the breaks?
- Read it again, taking a stanza each. What is the main idea in each stanza?
- Write out your stanza as a monologue for a) the sitter (stanza 1), b) the baby (stanza 2).

ACTIVITY 8

Work with a partner and consider 'Marged' (page 127).

a Copy the poem and highlight the parts about the poet in one colour and 'Marged' in another. Write down your ideas.

b Circle the pronouns in the poem. Add notes about these.

c Read the poem aloud and comment on the metre and rhyme scheme.

d Write a paragraph about the structure of this sonnet.

Stretch your skills

Copy the poem 'Coming Home'. Work with a partner to make annotations on the following:

- sound patterning and metre
- time scheme – past, present, future
- the different focus of each stanza
- how the stanzas are linked
- how the poet uses verbs and tenses
- connections between relationships, places, poetry and time.

Now write your own poem with the same title, trying to imitate Gillian Clarke's use of the above techniques. Imagine you have been away for a while and describe your journey as you see things with new eyes and think of people you have left.

Personal response

Gillian Clarke's poems can sometimes be shocking in the direct way they deal with pain, death, or the facts of life. Her viewpoint is always compassionate and humane, but she doesn't shy away from the harshness of nature or the difficulties of being a woman, a mother and a human being. She writes about childhood and the elusiveness of memory; about history and the land and our closeness to them, and about the possibilities of violent death, for both animals and people, because it is a part of life. Her poems can connect a single incident with a universal perspective.

ACTIVITY 9

Look at 'Overheard in County Sligo'. Group the quotations under 'Life now' or 'Might have been'.

> live in the back of beyond

> lie in the lap of the land

> work on the Abbey stage

> have my name in a book

> still the crowd with a look

> order and dust the tumbled rooms

Write a paragraph for each of your headings, giving the woman's feelings.

ACTIVITY 10

Work with a partner and choose one of Clarke's poems. Imagine that one of you is the poet herself and the other is a radio interviewer. Write and record the script of an interview with the poet about your chosen poem. Try to ask and answer the kind of questions that other students would find helpful.

Stretch your skills

Choose one of Clarke's poems and work with a partner to answer the following:

- What is the situation in the poem?
- What feelings are shown in the poem?
- How does the poet use language in the poem?
- What is the structure of the poem?
- How do each of the above help the reader to understand the poem?

Use your answers to prepare a leaflet on the poem, in which you try to persuade other students that it is a poem they should enjoy and take seriously. You should include pictures, quotations and your opinions.

CLARKE: SAMPLE TASKS

Sample task 1 (foundation level)

the girl's rescue from the lake

she remembers every detail of the scene years later

Poem: 'Cold Knap Lake'

Explore this **memory from childhood** that Clarke **recalls in such detail**.

comment on the different things she says

You should consider:

- what the poet sees – the details she remembers of the situation

- what the poet thinks – what she thought about at the time – and now

- the words and phrases the poet uses – how she writes about it using images and sound patterns, etc.

A good way to start is with an outline like this:

<u>Cold Knap Lake</u>

Situation:	child drowns in lake Clarke's mother gives kiss of life	What poet thinks:	'Was I there?' lost things in lake
What poet sees:	details of child – weeds, blue lips details of mother – red hair, cotton frock	Words and phrases she uses:	'long green silk' 'gave a stranger's child her breath'

You could add more notes with other details and quotations.

Then you could do a plan, so that you know what order you will write your answer in:

1. Describe the situation the poet is writing about. → 2. Describe what the poet remembers seeing in detail, with quotations to support what you say. → 3. Describe the poet's thoughts and feelings when she was a child at the scene, with quotations as evidence. ↓

6. Show how the poet connects the lake with the idea of memory being like water in which things get lost, using quotations as evidence. ← 5. Comment on the way the poet uses words and phrases to make the scene real and to show what she was and is thinking and feeling about the event, using quotations as evidence. ← 4. Describe the poet's thoughts and feelings about this memory as an adult, with quotations as evidence.

You could underline and number the quotations you want to use on the poem and link the numbers to your plan.

Sample task 2 (foundation level)

asking for an informed personal response

things that are different from 'tourist' view

What do **you** find **interesting or unusual** about the way Clarke shows **Welsh country life** in **EITHER** 'The Field-Mouse' **OR** 'Hare in July'.

You should consider

what you can imagine life is like from her poems

- the subjects the poet writes about
- the ways in which people and animals behave
- the words and phrases the poet uses in your chosen poem

things like harvests, death of animals, growing things

attitudes of people and animals to each other

pick out unusual thoughts or images; ideas about time or history; verbs and descriptions

Student response – Sample task I (foundation level)

The poem is about the time Gillian Clarke saw a drowned child. It was a little girl and her lips were blue. I know this because it says she was 'Blue-lipped'. Clarke also remembers how her mother's cotton frock was soaked. This was because the child was so wet. Her mother gave the child the kiss of life and she came round. The poem says she was 'bleating', which is like a lamb that is lost and that she was 'rosy' which means the colour was back in her cheeks.

Clarke thought her mother was a heroine because nobody else did anything to help the girl. Then her father took her home and she lived in a poor house and she got beaten for nearly dying which was not fair. I think her parents were worried and that's why they beat her.

Clarke cannot quite remember if she was really there or if she got told about it later. She talks about the bottom of the lake when mud gets stirred up by the swans' feet. I think she means this is like people's minds when something stirs up a memory, like seeing the drowned girl.

uses embedded quotations

relevance of comments not shown, but thoughtful ideas

good brief overview to start

some perceptive comments but not followed up

relevance of comments not shown, but thoughtful ideas

shows sound understanding of metaphor but does not use term

Student response – Sample task I (foundation level) continued

I like some of the images she uses, like talking about the weeds as 'the water's long green silk' which makes you think of a beautiful dress. I also think it's good where she says 'my mother gave a stranger's child her breath'. This was because her mother gave the child the kiss of life, which is literally giving her life again. I also like the description of the swans 'as their wings beat and whistle on the air' because this is how swans sound when they take off.

I think it is good the way the poem finishes with a rhyme about how lost things are in the lake with the drowned child. I think she means memories are lost and the mind is like the lake. Clarke uses alliteration here, 'lost things lie'.

Overall I think Clarke shows how hard it is to remember whether you really saw something as a child or not.

good choice of images used as quotations; well explained but not sufficiently evaluated

student identifies alliteration but fails to comment on its effects

some thoughtful comment on comparison, but little use of connotations

EXAMINER'S COMMENTS OCR
RECOGNISING ACHIEVEMENT

- The student shows a thoughtful personal response to the poem, and a good understanding of its content and some of the poet's language choices.
- For higher marks, more exploration and explanation of the student's ideas is needed, as well as an understanding of the effects of the literary techniques used.

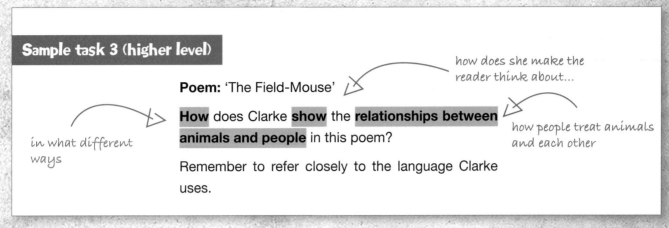

Sample task 3 (higher level)

how does she make the
reader think about...

Poem: 'The Field-Mouse'

How does Clarke **show** the **relationships between
animals and people** in this poem?

in what different
ways

how people treat animals
and each other

Remember to refer closely to the language Clarke
uses.

A good way to approach the question is to start with a spider diagram
which includes all the aspects you need to consider.

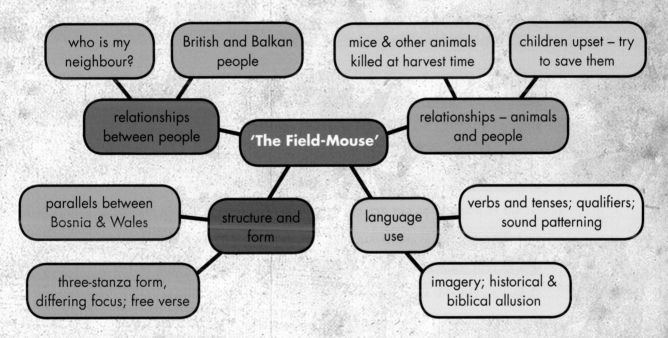

You could include more boxes with appropriate
quotations or you could underline the
quotations you wish to use and link them with
numbers to your boxes.

Then write a brief outline plan so that you know
the structure of your answer.

1. Start with a summary of the situation in
    the poem, showing how it is relevant to the
    question.
2. Write about the relationships the poet portrays
    between people and animals – perhaps adults
    and children have different ones.

3. Write about the relationships the poet
    shows between people; neighbours in Wales,
    neighbours in Bosnia (or any war).
4. Write about the way the writer uses parallels
    between the harvest in Wales and the killing
    in the Balkans. Is this helped by the free-
    verse form?
5. Write about the ways the writer uses language
    to make us see vivid images; associations
    with history (war) and references to the Bible
    about neighbours and land.
6. Give your personal response to the poem.

Sample task 4 (higher level)

What different ways does she show?

How does Clarke portray what **life is like for women** in **rural communities** in **EITHER** 'Overheard in County Sligo' **OR** 'The Hare'?

the hardships and rewards of being a wife, mother, friend, etc.

Remember to refer closely to the language Clarke uses in your chosen poem.

in the countryside, especially on a farm

Student response – Sample task 3 (higher level)

concise overview states main strands of poem

In the poem, Clarke and her family are harvesting hay with a machine. The blades are killing small mammals nesting in the field. While they are doing this there is 'the radio's terrible news' about a civil war taking place in Bosnia. Clarke uses this as a parallel situation throughout the poem.

perceptive point about animals in 'human domains'

The relationships she depicts between people and animals show that the animals stand little chance. She uses the poignant image of a child with 'his hands a nest of quivering mouse' to show how the children are upset by the slaughter. The phrase 'agony big as itself' shows the creature's suffering and the poet shows her feelings by writing 'the star goes out in its eye', which relates the mouse to universal pain and death.

point about children's feelings; comment on imagery

a thoughtful insight into the way the mouse is symbolic

well-chosen quotation relates harvest to war

The scale of the destruction is shown in 'the field lies bleeding', a phrase that could apply equally well to the massacres in Bosnia, or in other countries. The children have saved some animals which, like refugees, inhabit 'the dusk garden'. The adults may feel compassion for the animals, but they know the harvest must be gathered so there is food for the winter.

well-made points about 'refugees' and different view of adults.

Student response – Sample task 3 (higher level) continued

Clarke shows the relationships between people when she mentions 'our neighbour' and his 'chance gift of sweetness'. At the end of the poem she shows what can happen in a civil war 'my neighbour turned/stranger' as happened in Bosnia. The poet knows that humans are all part of one race, as she says 'we can't face the newspapers' because even 'a rumour of pain' can set people against each other.

Clarke's poem progresses from the hay cutting, through the deaths of creatures to a dream where 'the children dance in grass'. They are compared to the dead mammals through 'bones brittle as mouse-ribs', the alliteration creating a snapping sound, which is followed by 'the air/stammering with gunfire' which connects with the jets in stanza one.

The idea of 'Summer in Europe' suggests that all farmers should be getting in the harvest, but there is no let up in the fighting in Bosnia.

understanding of poet's use of neighbour; could have been developed more

fluent use of embedded quotations throughout

knowledge of technique; analysis and evaluation of quotations

intelligent analysis of structure – shows how it aids meaning

conclusion uses quotation to refer to and extend introduction

EXAMINER'S COMMENTS OCR

- In this answer, the student discusses the language used in the poem and how it creates particular effects. Comments are well-supported with apt textual evidence.
- A good Higher Tier response, but further development of ideas may produce a better result.

Wendy Cope, one of Britain's most popular poets, was born in Kent in 1945. After studying history at Oxford University, she worked as a primary school teacher and editor, before becoming a full-time writer. Her poetry collections, *Making Cocoa for Kingsley Amis*, *Serious Concerns*, *If I Don't Know* and *Two Cures for Love* are characterized by her wit and insight. The poet Ted Hughes praised her for 'whacking the nail on the head – when everybody else is trying to hang pictures on it'.

First impressions

Wendy Cope has said:

> 'I do believe that humour and powerful emotion can exist in the same poem. And that a funny poem can be saying something important.'

Wendy Cope is mainly regarded as a writer of comic or 'light' verse. But beneath the playfulness of her poems, serious points are often being made. 'Lonely Hearts' (page 141) at first appears to be a parody of 'lonely hearts' classified advertisements, but its plaintive repetition of 'Is it you?' suggests a near-universal loneliness. As you read Cope's poems, look closely for the sources of both humour and powerful emotions.

ACTIVITY 1

Quickly look through Cope's poems and identify the following:

- a poem written as two letters
- a poem about a fish
- poems with 'Strugnell' in the title
- poems that start with a quotation or epigraph
- poems about jobs
- poems about love.

With a partner, discuss your first impressions of the topics and style of Cope's poetry.

Cope frequently refers to the work of other writers. In order to understand these references, you should read widely. One particular influence and inspiration is the poet Philip Larkin (1922–1985.) The poem 'Mr Strugnell' (page 144) is based on Larkin's poem 'Mr Bleaney,' and on Larkin's own life. In his poem 'Annus Mirabilis', Larkin wrote 'Sexual intercourse began/ In nineteen sixty-three.' How does Cope refer to this in the fifth stanza of her poem? Larkin worked as a librarian in Hull. How does Cope use this information? Research the life and work of Philip Larkin and consider its effect on Cope's writing.

ACTIVITY 2

Look at the statements below from Cope's poems and, with a partner, discuss your impression of the speaker:

'I am sustained by the belief that I am ahead of my time.'

'Yes, life is hard if you choose engineering.'

'Your taste's too highbrow for me, Mrs M.'

Imagery

Some of Cope's poems avoid traditional poetic use of figurative language. In 'Reading Scheme' (page 146) she chooses instead the simple diction and syntax of a primary school reading book to disguise a more adult and dangerous message. However other poems, such as 'Sonnet of '68' (page 147) and 'The Lavatory Attendant' (page 148), use imagery in rich and varied ways. In some poems Cope uses books, poetry and even classified advertisements to symbolize the challenges of communication and relationships.

ACTIVITY 3

Read 'The Lavatory Attendant' (page 148) and complete the grid below:

	Poetic technique	Explanation
'His face is overripe Wensleydale/ Going blue at the edges'	Metaphor	The attendant's face is compared to Yorkshire cheese. 'Overripe' and 'blue' sound unhealthy.
'a row of fonts'		
'lids like eye-patches'		
'Short-lived Niagaras'		
'Turns Medusa on her head'		

ACTIVITY 4

What do you think the following symbolize in Cope's poems:

- Poets' Corner in Westminster Abbey (pictured here)
- the dead stickleback
- being picked last for games
- 1968
- 'lonely hearts' advertisements?

Choose one and prepare a presentation explaining its significance in one of the poems.

Stretch your skills

In 'Exchange of Letters' (page 139) Cope personifies a poem and a novel to suggest two specific, contrasting personalities. Consider how the 'voices' of the poem and the novel are established. What does the reader learn about the poem's past love life? What clues do we receive that the novel is pretentious, unsuccessful and self-centred? How self-aware do you think the poem and novel are?

Using the flow chart below, write your own personification poem:

Object ➔ Personality ➔ Clues to reader

Evaluate how well you have captured the 'voice' of your object.

Language

Cope's use of rhyme contributes greatly to the style and impact of her poems. In 'Message' (page 143) the reader anticipates each end-rhyme (rhyming alternately with either 'late' or 'spare') only to be brought up short by the final line, which rhymes with neither – instead, it contains the abrupt command 'Pick up the phone'.

Cope also uses alliteration (such as 'ballads… blueprints', page 138), assonance and consonance. Her language conveys a keen sense of time and place; consider her specific choice of place names, from Yalding to Tulse Hill. Her language conjures up train journeys, schools and English gardens.

ACTIVITY 5

'Sonnet of '68' (page 147) is a translation of a German poem written about student protests, which sometimes ended violently. Look carefully at the language used and complete the grid below.

Feature	Examples from poem
Rhyming words	First two stanzas are *abba*, but then pattern changes. Change in mood?
Use of alliteration	'fight/ For freedom'
Unfamiliar words (look up their meanings)	'Utopian': an ideal society
Words that sound violent	
Words that sound quiet or defeated	

ACTIVITY 6

Cope's use of language often highlights 'ordinariness'.

'I had a slight cold but it's better today.'

'I am no beauty but I'm pretty smart.'

'Just bear in mind that you are forty-eight.'

With a partner, discuss how Cope's choice of language in these poems is different from that of other poems you have read.

Stretch your skills

Cope has invented a poet, Jason Strugnell, who writes in the style of many other poets. In the two Strugnell's Sonnets in your Anthology, Cope borrows and adapts the first line of Shakespearean sonnets. 'Strugnell's Sonnets (iv)' is inspired by Shakespeare's Sonnet 55, which begins: 'Not marble, nor the gilded monuments/ Of princes, shall outlive this powerful rhyme.'

'Strugnell's Sonnets (vii)' alters the first line of Shakespeare's Sonnet 110: 'Alas, 'tis true I have gone here and there/ And made myself a motley to the view.'

What are the similarities and differences between Strugnell's and Shakespeare's language?

Structure

Cope frequently writes in established poetic forms, such as villanelles and sonnets. Her villanelles, such as 'Reading Scheme', 'Manifesto' and 'Lonely Hearts' contain five stanzas of tercets (three lines) and a concluding quatrain (four lines) in which the alternate final lines are brought together, increasing the impact of the repeated refrains. Her sonnets use both the Shakespearean form ('Strugnell's Sonnets') and the Petrarchan form ('Sonnet of '68').

Although Cope is renowned for her handling of rhyme and metre, she experiments with freer forms in some of her poems, such as 'On Finding an Old Photograph' and 'Exchange of Letters'.

ACTIVITY 7

Both the villanelles and the Shakespearean sonnets end in rhyming couplets. Look at the poems below and write a paragraph explaining the effect of the concluding rhyming couplet:

- 'Reading Scheme'
- 'Lonely Hearts'
- 'Strugnell's Sonnets (iv)'

Consider whether the final couplet surprises the reader or reinforces an idea that is developed in the poem.

ACTIVITY 8

'The Stickleback Song' (page 149), as its title suggests, resembles a song with its strong rhythm, rhyme and use of repetition. Read it aloud and mark the syllables that you think should be stressed. Experiment with reading the poem as a group.

How does the use of rhythm and repetition increase your enjoyment of this poem?

Stretch your skills

Villanelles are an exciting and challenging verse form. Use the spider diagram opposite to plan your own villanelle.

Now write five three-line stanzas, each with an *aba* rhyme scheme. Conclude with a final quatrain with an *abaa* structure. Compare your work with other famous villanelles, such as Dylan Thomas's 'Do Not Go Gentle Into That Good Night'. Why do you think Cope and other poets are attracted to this form?

First refrain   Second refrain

Subject of villanelle

'a' rhyming words   'b' rhyming words

Personal response

Cope writes on themes such as love, loneliness, art, and outsiders, using a variety of forms and styles. You may be amused by 'The Stickleback Song' (written in response to an inspector's comment when Cope was a teacher) or moved by the plight of 'Tich Miller'. 'Manifesto', 'Lonely Hearts', 'Message' and 'Exchange of Letters' all deal with the search for love, but you may find some more humorous and others more poignant.

Cope values the art of writing. Do you agree with her defence of poets in 'Engineers' Corner'? Or do you side with Strugnell, whose 'verse is rotten'?

ACTIVITY 10

Two characters that Cope depicts are Tich Miller and Mr Strugnell. Complete the grid below to analyse how they are presented.

	Tich Miller	Mr Strugnell
Description	'glasses/ with elastoplast-pink frames'	'quiet sort'
Setting	School	Boarding house and 'lumpy, single bed'
Language	'lolloped, unselected'	
Change	Changes schools	'much more relaxed'
Ending		

With which character do you feel more sympathy, and why?

ACTIVITY 9

Look at the two portrayals of love below and write a speech explaining which you like the most.

From 'Being Boring':

'safe mooring'

'A happier cabbage you never did see'

'Someone to stay home with was all my desire'

From 'Manifesto':

'You're always on my mind when we're apart'

'And write the poems that will win your heart'

Stretch your skills

Cope's work contains many literary references. To increase your understanding and appreciation of her poetry, research the following writers and their work. Annotate your Anthology explaining why you think she has referred to these particular writers or literary texts.

- In 'Strugnell's Sonnets (vii)': 'Edward Thomas, Yeats or Pound'; 'Andrew Motion'; 'you'll be lonelier than any cloud' (William Wordsworth).
- In 'Mr Strugnell': 'Pam Ayres'; 'Patience Strong'.
- In 'The Lavatory Attendant': Coleridge. Also research Craig Raine, as this poem is a parody of his 'Yellow Pages' poems.

Create a presentation explaining how Cope conveys the importance of poetry.

COPE: SAMPLE TASKS

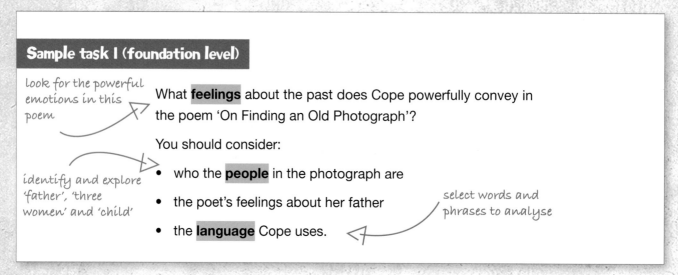

Sample task I (foundation level)

look for the powerful emotions in this poem

What **feelings** about the past does Cope powerfully convey in the poem 'On Finding an Old Photograph'?

You should consider:

identify and explore 'father', 'three women' and 'child'

- who the **people** in the photograph are
- the poet's feelings about her father
- the **language** Cope uses.

select words and phrases to analyse

Spend time planning your response to the poem. It is tempting to write simply about the reaction to the father, but you must be sure to include a discussion of language, structure and form and explain how this helps to create the mood and meaning of this poem.

Use the grid below to help you plan a discussion of the poem's features.

Structure	Five stanzas. First four are three-line stanzas. Fifth has only one line.
Form	Non-rhyming, free verse.
Language: alliteration, assonance, consonance?	
Imagery: metaphors, similes, symbolism?	

There are many ways that you could order and organize your response. You may wish to use the bullet points as guidance and make a plan based on the flow chart below.

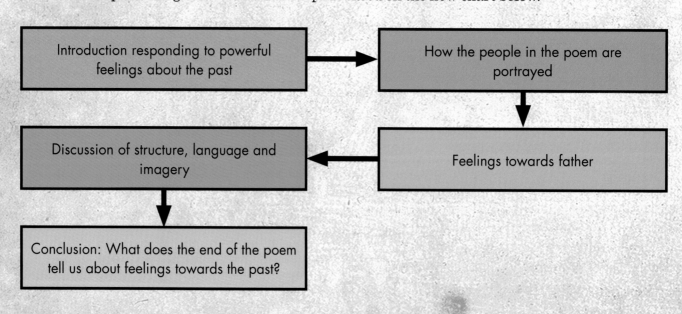

Introduction responding to powerful feelings about the past → How the people in the poem are portrayed

Discussion of structure, language and imagery ← Feelings towards father

Conclusion: What does the end of the poem tell us about feelings towards the past?

Or you may choose, after your introductory paragraph, to work your way through the poem, stanza by stanza. But if you do this, make sure that you don't run out of time and neglect the end of the poem.

Sample task 2 (foundation level)

what makes you feel sorry for Tich Miller?

choose words that show how she is described and what happens to her

What do you find **moving** in the poem 'Tich Miller'?

Remember to **refer closely** to the **words and phrases** Cope uses.

include comments on language, structure and form

Student response – Sample task 1 (foundation level)

'On Finding an Old Photograph' is clearly about the past. The title suggests that this 'old' photograph has been found long after it was originally taken and the speaker is seeing it for the first time. The first two words 'Yalding, 1912' give it a place and date, perhaps suggesting that this phrase was written on the photograph itself. Throughout the poem, Cope is exploring the emotions that she feels towards her father, who is captured in this photograph when he was much younger and apparently happy.

shows an understanding of the whole poem and begins to answer question

The poem is written in five unrhymed stanzas of free verse, which suits its gentle, reflective nature, gradually revealing the photograph and her emotions about it to the reader. The first four stanzas are three lines each, while in the last, a single line stands on its own but delivers the powerful impact of Cope's sad realization about her relationship with her father.

sensitive discussion of structure and its effect

clearly responds to question

The first person mentioned in the poem is her father. Cope uses pathetic fallacy to reinforce the idea of her father's happiness.

uses correct terminology

He is in 'sunlight' in an 'apple orchard' with the word 'stylish' adding glamour to his image.

considers portrayal of father, using evidence from text – could this be expanded?

The other figures in the poem are more mysterious. The 'three women' may be other relations of Cope's, but they are not differentiated or named. The repeated consonance of 's' sounds in 'blouses', 'skirts', 'brush' and 'grass' lend a sleepy, soothing mood to this stanza. The unnamed 'child with curly hair' is an attractive addition adding to its dream-like quality.

well-selected evidence – attempts to describe mood

considers emotions

Cope is powerfully affected by this photograph, using the metaphor 'half-drugged' to describe its calming atmosphere. However, she has a more complex reaction because the figures are not 'strangers' to her. The reader learns that her relationship with her father was not easy: he experienced 'sadness' and she painfully recalls 'the things I didn't give him.'

good point, but could explain further

considers structure and its effect

The final line is a stanza on its own, which gives it more emphasis, and powerfully portrays the regret that Cope feels that her father appears only to be happy when she is 'unborn'. This suggests that she blames herself for his 'sadness'.

could possibly connect explicitly with question

EXAMINER'S COMMENTS OCR

- The student shows a good understanding of the issues explored in the poem and of technical terms and literary techniques.
- This is a strong Foundation Tier answer. For a better result, it requires further analysis and explanation, supported with good examples from the text.

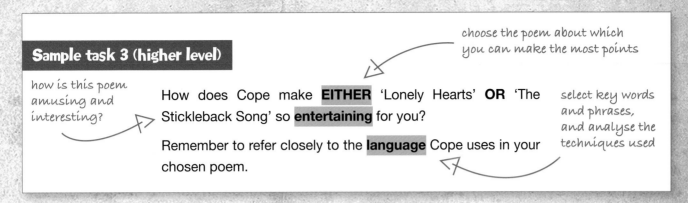

Sample task 3 (higher level)

choose the poem about which you can make the most points

how is this poem amusing and interesting?

How does Cope make **EITHER** 'Lonely Hearts' **OR** 'The Stickleback Song' so **entertaining** for you?

Remember to refer closely to the **language** Cope uses in your chosen poem.

select key words and phrases, and analyse the techniques used

Either 'The Stickleback Song' or 'Lonely Hearts' would make an excellent choice for this question. However, make sure that you choose one that you can *analyse* rather than simply the one that most amuses you. Look at the two sample student responses below and decide which you think is better:

Response 1:

The poem 'The Stickleback Song' is entertaining because it shows you the silly things people say. All the repetition makes me laugh.

Response 2:

In 'The Stickleback Song', Cope uses the repetition of the 'dead stickleback' refrain to highlight the absurdity of the inspector. The reader looks forward to the development through the stanzas as Cope wonders if there is a 'spectre' of a stickleback or perhaps the inspector's mind is about to 'crack'.

To support your ideas about the poems, you need to choose specific quotations and then explain how they contribute to making the poem entertaining. Read the quotations below and then write a sample paragraph including them and explaining their importance.

Quotation	How this makes the poem entertaining
'pronounced it OK'	Surprises the reader with informality – reports are usually formal
'we've got some gerbils, all thumping their tails'	
'We haven't a quick or a dead stickleback'	
'The ghost of some poor classroom pet'	
'You won't lose your wits for a few years, touch wood'	

Sample task 4 (higher level)

look for words and phrases that stand out

How does Cope **memorably portray** people's **disappointing** lives in **EITHER** 'Sonnet of '68' **OR** 'Being Boring'?

choose the poem about which you can make the most points

how have youthful passions changed?

Student response – Sample task 3 (higher level)

Wendy Cope uses a variety of techniques to entertain and interest the reader in her villanelle 'Lonely Hearts'. The poem is inspired by classified advertisements and contains a series of short pleas from a wide variety of people in North London looking for love and wondering 'Is it you?'

The reader is first entertained by Cope's parody of the style of these advertisements. They can imagine the meaning beneath the male biker's wish for 'touring fun' or the executive who wants 'something new'. The quests for love are not entirely idealized as concern with money ('solvent') and appearance ('with photo') shows that this is not just a purely emotional meeting of lonely hearts. Cope uses alliteration, for example, the unlikely coupling of 'Shakespeare and the sun' to emphasize how the lonely hearts must attempt to capture the interest of others in these advertisements. A more business-like and apparently unambitious ad again uses alliteration: 'Successful, straight and solvent'. This advertiser, perhaps after previous bad experiences, is hoping to attract a more conventional and conservative candidate.

confidently identifies form

discusses connotations with insight

confident use of literary terminology

some evidence of personal response

concisely sums up poem, demonstrating understanding

subtle points, well supported with brief examples

well-supported example

Student response – Sample task 3 (higher level) continued

The variety of the advertisers adds to the humour of the poem. What could the 'Libran, inexperienced and blue' have in common with the more adventurous-sounding bikers and executives? There are also suggestions of sadder stories, such as the 'Attractive Jewish lady with a son'. The highlighting of her religion and child contrasts with the desired 'bisexual woman, arty, young'.

must be careful not to wander from question

The villanelle form of the poem greatly adds to its entertainment. The regular 'aba' rhyme scheme leads the reader to anticipate each end-rhyme. Each line either rhymes with the word 'true' or 'fun', so Cope's clever variety of rhymes increases the poem's interest. The repeated refrains 'Do you live in North London? Is it you?' and 'Can someone make my simple wish come true?' are questions and there are a total of 14 questions in the poem. The repetition of these questions builds to a poignant and powerful final rhyming couplet, suggesting that there are thousands of people all lonely and seeking love. Perhaps this is not such a 'simple wish' after all?

confident use of technical terms

insight into language and form

discusses how form contributes to entertainment, so returns well to question

an insightful reading of the poem

EXAMINER'S COMMENTS OCR

RECOGNISING ACHIEVEMENT

- In this response, the student shows insight into the poem and a confident grasp of language choices.
- Quotations chosen from the text are particularly apt.
- While this is a good answer, it could be improved with further evidence of personal response, as well as greater focus.

Carol Ann Duffy, one of Britain's best known and most respected poets, was born in Glasgow in 1955. She has written a number of acclaimed collections of poetry including *Mean Time*, *The World's Wife* and *Rapture*. Her subjects include childhood, love and memory. In 2009 she was the first woman to be appointed Poet Laureate, and in this role she has written poems on topics ranging from David Beckham's injured foot to volcanic ash.

First impressions

Carol Ann Duffy has said:

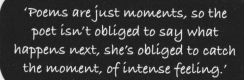

'Poems are just moments, so the poet isn't obliged to say what happens next, she's obliged to catch the moment, of intense feeling.'

When reading her poems for the first time, try to identify both the moment Duffy is capturing and the emotions she is exploring. Some of her poems deal directly with her own life, while others are **dramatic monologues** exploring the feelings of other people, real or imagined. Her titles are often short, such as 'Liar' or 'Answer', perhaps surprising the reader with their bluntness. As a poet, Duffy is interested in form, so you must explore how her poems look on the page, as well as how they sound when read aloud.

ACTIVITY I

Both 'Head of English' (page 155) and 'In Mrs Tilscher's Class' (page 156) are about teachers. What are your first impressions of these two poems?

	'Head of English'	'In Mrs Tilscher's Class'
Who is the speaker in the poem?		
What key words or phrases are used?		
What patterns can you find in the poem?		
What is the poet's attitude to the teacher in the poem?		
Which poem do you prefer, and why?		

Memory and childhood are frequent themes in Duffy's poems. 'The Good Teachers' (page 162) cheerfully celebrates her school days, while 'Brothers' (page 153) is a more sombre layering of memories of her brothers as boys, who, she predicts, will become the men who will eventually carry her coffin. Choose a childhood memory of your own and use the spider diagram below to help plan your own poem.

Using the first stanza of 'In Mrs Tilscher's Class' as a guide, try forming your memory into a poem.

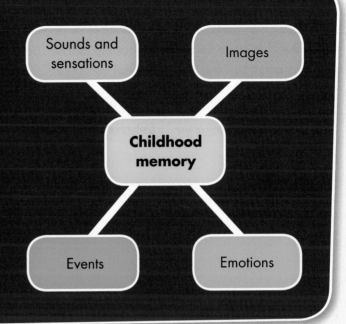

Sounds and sensations

Images

Childhood memory

Events

Emotions

Imagery

Carol Ann Duffy uses a rich and wide range of imagery to convey intense emotions in her poems. Winter imagery is employed in 'Stealing' (page 161) and 'Wintering' (page 165) to express emotions which are cold or bleak. This contrasts with the 'feverish July' of Duffy's childhood depicted in 'In Mrs Tilscher's Class' (page 156) or the melancholy autumn of 'In Your Mind' (page 157). Religious imagery, perhaps reflecting Duffy's own Catholic childhood, features in several poems, such as 'The War Photographer' (page 163). When reading the poems, identify not only the techniques used but the feelings they suggest to you.

ACTIVITY 2

What are your first impressions of these poems based on their first lines?

- 'You were dead, but we met, dreaming'
- 'The most unusual thing I ever stole? A snowman.'
- 'I worry about you travelling in those mystical machines'

Write a paragraph comparing the mood and tone of these openings.

ACTIVITY 3

'Wintering' (page 165) uses a number of poetic techniques to convey the sorrow at the end of a love affair. Look at the phrases below and identify the techniques used and their effect on the reader.

Quotation	Poetic technique	Effect on reader
'the small stiff body of my phone'	Metaphor	Compares silent phone to a corpse. Reminds reader of lack of communication and the death of love.
'Bare trees hold out their arms, beseech, entreat'		
'they play inside my head like broken chords'		
'The wind screams at the house, bitter, betrayed'		
'your footprints like a love letter below'		

Language

'Remember/ the lesson on assonance, for not all poems,/ sadly, rhyme these days.' Duffy has the unsympathetic and conventional 'Head of English' (page 155) express a lack of appreciation for modern poetry and, one assumes, the work of Duffy herself. Duffy's poems do sometimes use rhyme, as well as alliteration, onomatopoeia and assonance. Her use of colloquial language and conversational diction in some poems increases the sense of intimacy and accessibility. The best way to experience her rich use of language is to read the poems aloud, paying special attention to the sound of the words.

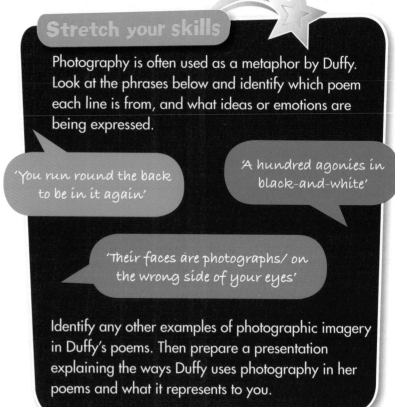

Stretch your skills

Photography is often used as a metaphor by Duffy. Look at the phrases below and identify which poem each line is from, and what ideas or emotions are being expressed.

'You run round the back to be in it again'

'A hundred agonies in black-and-white'

'Their faces are photographs/ on the wrong side of your eyes'

Identify any other examples of photographic imagery in Duffy's poems. Then prepare a presentation explaining the ways Duffy uses photography in her poems and what it represents to you.

ACTIVITY 4

Look at 'Head of English' and find which words rhyme with the following:

Word	Rhyming word
bounds	
forth	
go	
view	
reams	

Can you find a pattern to the rhyming, or is it irregular? Do all the rhymes occur at the ends of lines, or are there some internal rhymes? Why do you think Duffy uses rhymes in this poem?

ACTIVITY 5

Look at the examples below of onomatopoeia from Duffy's poems, and experiment with different ways of reading these phrases:

- 'fizzy, movie tomorrows'
- 'howled, shrieked, clawed'
- 'swish down the corridor'

Find other examples from the poems and then write a paragraph explaining how the use of onomatopoeia makes the poems more vivid for the reader.

Structure

All of Duffy's poems in the Anthology are written in stanzas, with the majority being between four and six stanzas long, with four to eight lines in each stanza. Most of her poems avoid regular use of rhyme, but she shapes her ideas in other ways such as by the use of repetition and regular line lengths. Although formally presented on the page in even lines and stanzas, the poems use techniques such as enjambment and internal punctuation to create a freer, more conversational rhythm.

Stretch your skills

Alliteration is an easy poetic technique to spot, but it is difficult to explain. Why is 'shrunk size of a snapshot' better than 'reduced size of a tiny picture'? Does a repeated sibilant 's' create a different impression from a plosive 'b' or dental 'd'? Look at the student response below and see how you would extend this explanation of alliteration in 'Liar' (page 158).

In 'Liar', the alliterative phrase 'falsehood, fiction, fib' has a repeated 'f' sound which forms words that can be spat out like accusations at the liar in the poem.

ACTIVITY 6

In 'Answer' (page 151) Duffy uses repetition to produce a complex image of a lover. Complete the spider diagram below to explore the effect of each stanza and then answer the questions underneath.

- What key phrases are repeated?
- What impression does the reader have of the loved one?
- What is the question to which the answer is 'yes, yes'?

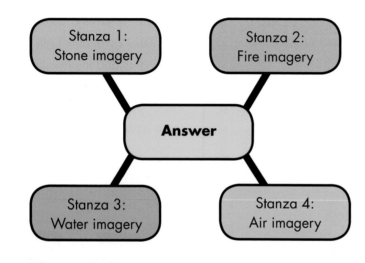

Stanza 1:
Stone imagery

Stanza 2:
Fire imagery

Answer

Stanza 3:
Water imagery

Stanza 4:
Air imagery

ACTIVITY 7

Some of Duffy's poems, such as 'Stealing' (page 161), 'Mrs Lazarus' (page 159) and 'Head of English' (page 155) are dramatic monologues in which the speaker clearly is not the poet herself. Read each of these poems carefully, highlighting any examples you find of the following:

- enjambment
- short, blunt sentences
- full stops or semi-colons in the middle of a line.

How do these structural features help us to understand the poem's speaker?

Stretch your skills

Duffy often highlights her interest in the themes of time and memory through the structure of her poems. In some, there is a sense that something has happened between the stanzas. For example, in 'Wintering' (page 165) there are asterisks between some stanzas. What does that suggest to you? Has there been a shift in time or mood? Explain what you think has happened between the following stanzas:

- between stanzas four and five in 'Head of English'
- between stanzas two and three in 'In Mrs Tilscher's Class'
- between stanzas three and four in 'War Photographer'.

Personal response

Duffy's poems are about deep feelings, and they often inspire deep feelings in those who read them. Whether grieving over a lost love, recalling a happy moment from childhood, or mourning a death, she uses poetry to shape intense emotions into a form which will resonate with the reader. Some poems, such as 'Head of English' or 'Liar' may amuse or surprise you, while others, such as 'Wintering' or 'Dream of a Lost Friend' may make you sad. As you read her poems, highlight any words or phrases which you find striking and think about the effect they have on you.

ACTIVITY 8

Duffy considers many aspects of love in her poetry. Look at the quotations below and try to identify the type of love being portrayed and your personal response.

Quotation	Type of love	Personal response
'I wanted the bold girl'	Daughter's love for her mother	
'the answer is yes, yes'		
'she'd left a good gold star'		
'sweet pain in the heart'		
'that trick we have of turning love to pain'		

ACTIVITY 9

The poet's choice of speaker, form, diction and language will influence your personal response to the poem. Use the spider diagram below to record your response to the poem 'Stealing'.

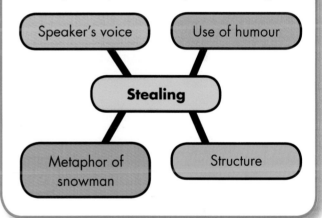

Stretch your skills

Your personal response to 'Mrs Lazarus' will be influenced by your knowledge of the story from St John's gospel, which depicts the miraculous resurrection of Lazarus four days after his death. Read this passage from the Bible and compare it to Duffy's poem. Why has Duffy chosen to tell this story from the point of view of Mrs Lazarus?

There are some similarities between this poem and the short story 'The Monkey's Paw' by W.W. Jacobs. What is your response to the horror of the ending of both the poem and the short story?

DUFFY: SAMPLE TASKS

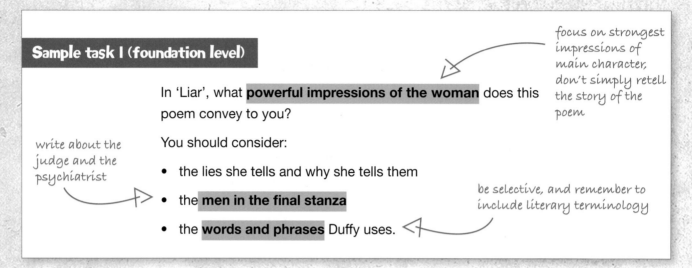

Sample task I (foundation level)

In 'Liar', what **powerful impressions of the woman** does this poem convey to you?

focus on strongest impressions of main character, don't simply retell the story of the poem

You should consider:

write about the judge and the psychiatrist

- the lies she tells and why she tells them
- the **men in the final stanza**
- the **words and phrases** Duffy uses.

be selective, and remember to include literary terminology

It is important that you take a few minutes to plan and organize your response. Use the spider diagram below to begin your planning.

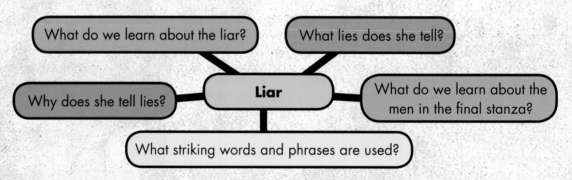

As you write your response, it is important to keep in mind the Assessment Objectives for this examination. Even though the question does not specifically ask you about form, structure or literary techniques, it is important that you include your understanding of how the writer uses these to present the 'Liar' in this poem.

In preparing your response to the question about 'Liar' you might use the grid below:

	Evidence	Explanation
Impact of title	'Liar'	Single word labels the woman unsympathetically
Structure and progression of stanzas	Four stanzas, each of six lines	
Lines in italics		
Use of metaphor		
Use of alliteration		
Presentation of male characters		
Impact of final stanza		

Sample task 2 (foundation level)

What powerful impressions of school life do **EITHER** 'In Mrs Tilscher's Class' **OR** 'The Good Teachers' convey to you?

You should consider:

- the teacher(s) and **the way the pupils feel about them**
- the changes in the **pupils as they develop**
- the **words and phrases** Duffy uses in your chosen poem.

What emotions and feelings are explored?

Highlight striking words and phrases. Remember to note literary techniques.

Consider structure. Is there a point in the poem when changes occur?

Student response – Sample task 1 (foundation level)

In 'Liar', Carol Ann Duffy creates a powerful image of a woman who lies constantly, perhaps to escape her dull 'humdrum' life. Some of her fantasies appear harmless, while others seem more odd and dangerous. Her lies may be based on her secret dreams, memories and hopes, yet they lead to tragedy.

The first powerful impression of the woman in the poem is suggested by the single-word title 'Liar'. This creates an unsympathetic image, and many other words about lying are used such as the alliterative phrase 'falsehood, fiction, fib.' In the first stanza, the lies deal with the woman's identity as she claims to be a man and switches her 'floral/ day-frock' for 'heavy herringbone.' These alliterative phrases suggest a feminine identity transforming into a masculine one. The reader also learns the woman's name, 'Susan', which is almost comically ordinary given her complex personality.

In the second stanza, Duffy may surprise the reader by suggesting that she 'lived like you do'. The metaphor of the 'dozen slack rope-ends' evokes the many unfulfilled dreams and

responds to question, repeating some key words

discusses language and provides examples

could mention the use of second person

what other points could be made about this?

confident use of literary term and explains point well

Student response – Sample task I (foundation level) continued

fantasies that we may all have. Her more harmless lies, like those about nearly drowning or living in Moscow, seem attempts to add glamour or excitement to an otherwise dull life.

evidence of personal response to poem

In the final stanza, however, things go 'From bad to worse' and Duffy suggests that the woman has 'stolen' a child. Her lies are no longer simply 'Hyperbole, falsehood, fiction, fib' or private fantasies, for which Duffy uses the metaphor 'secret films'. She has now taken dangerous and illegal action.

mentions stanzas, but could say more about structure

good use of terminology, but could explain effect more

However, the men in the final stanza are presented as being just as deluded as the woman. The judge is described as 'The man in the long white wig', emphasizing his old-fashioned appearance rather than his legal knowledge. More surprisingly, the psychiatrist who sends her to 'gaol' acts out fantasies about the 'Princess of Wales' when he gets home. The men who judge the woman are just as sadly confused as she is, which may make the reader feel more sympathetic about her need to lie.

opportunity to discuss tone and message of poem; perhaps return more clearly to question?

EXAMINER'S COMMENTS OCR

- The student shows some knowledge of the poem and of literary terminology.
- Throughout the response, however, ideas are underdeveloped, leaving the reader hanging. More explanation and insight is needed for higher marks.

Sample task 3 (higher level)

look for positive and negative imagery

How does Duffy memorably convey to you the **pains and pleasures** of being in love in **EITHER** 'Wintering' **OR** 'Answer'?

choose the poem you know best and about which you can make the most points

Remember to refer closely to **the language Duffy uses** in your chosen poem.

select key words and phrases and remember to use correct literary terminology

Either 'Answer' or 'Wintering' would be excellent poems to discuss for this question, so you should base your choice on deciding which one enables you to make the most interesting points. The examiner is looking for answers which respond 'critically and imaginatively' to the poems.

To make your initial decision, use the two spider diagrams below.

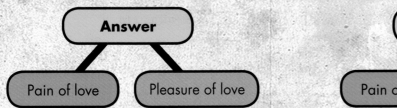

It is vital that you select key words and phrases to support your ideas when answering this question. Look at the quotations below from the two poems and complete the grid.

Quotation	Literary technique	Point about the pain or pleasure of love
'your head a wild Medusa hissing flame'	Metaphor	This love seems dangerous, frightening and painful. Medusa is a monstrous image, but also used by some feminist writers to suggest female empowerment.
'your fingers burning pungent brands on flesh'		
'your arms a whirlpool spinning me around'		
'I wear a shroud of cold beneath my clothes'		
'The wind screams at the house'		
'your flower kiss'		

possibility to contrast brothers as boys and adults

look for imagery used to convey the past

How does Duffy portray **the power of memory** in **EITHER 'Brothers' OR 'Nostalgia'**?

what memories are important?

Refer closely to **Duffy's use of language** in your chosen poem.

consider repetition, diction and imagery

Student response – Sample task 3 (higher level)

In 'Wintering', Carol Ann Duffy uses a wide range of poetic techniques to convey both the bitter pain of love lost and the fragile, pleasurable hope of love regained. The title of the poem sets the poem in the depth of winter and Duffy uses pathetic fallacy to portray the cold, bleak despair when love has vanished.

refers directly to question

concise introduction and begins making points immediately

Throughout the 12 stanzas, the poem traces the despair of the speaker with a series of desolate images. The poem is divided into three sections separated by asterisks, which suggests a passage of time and heightens the slow progress of the poem. In the first section, death is suggested when 'slow funerals have ploughed the rain' and death imagery continues with 'a shroud of cold' and 'the small stiff body of my phone'. The speaker seems entirely alone and the corpse and funeral imagery reinforce this sense of isolation and desolation.

considers structure and explains effect

selects evidence from text

In the second section of the poem, Duffy employs nature imagery to intensify the sense of despair. The garden is personified and mirrors the speaker's depression by weeping and lying face down, grieving. The trees are also given human characteristics as they 'hold out their arms, beseech, entreat'. This pathetic fallacy vividly presents the speaker's anguish and the

discusses the pain of love

confident use of literary terminology

explains effect thoroughly

Student response – Sample task 3 (higher level) continued

use of assonance, repeating the vowel 'e,' creates a shrieking, pleading sound. This section is raw with emotion and heightens the sense of pain resulting from lost love. The alliteration in the plosive phrase 'bitter, betrayed' seems to bite with anger.

detailed discussion of the pain of love

However, the third section of the poem is gentler and the imagery becomes lighter. The simile 'your footprints like a love letter' suggests a sense of reconciliation or hope. The winter imagery is replaced by spring which 'blurts in green'. Pain seems to be replaced by the pleasure of 'your flower kiss' and the poem ends on an optimistic note, just as spring brings a welcome end to winter. The last stanza begins 'as pain turns back again to love', reminding the reader of the first stanza's 'that trick we have of turning love to pain', suggesting that love, like the seasons, is cyclical.

confident use of literary term

sensitive interpretation

considers the pleasure of love

shows understanding of the whole poem

EXAMINER'S COMMENTS OCR

- This response presents a strong understanding of the whole poem, clearly focused on the question throughout and with sophisticated use of quotation and reference to technical terms.
- The student writes with confidence and insight.
- An extremely good answer, doing as much as could be reasonably expected under exam conditions.

Seamus Heaney was born in 1939, the son of a farmer and the eldest of nine children. When he was 12 he won a scholarship to a school in Derry followed by a degree from Queen's University in Belfast. He is married to Marie Devlin and the couple have three children. Heaney was Professor of Poetry at Oxford, and now holds a prestigious part-time post at the University of California. He has lived through the troubles in Ireland, and has a cottage in Wicklow where he writes. Heaney was awarded the Nobel Prize for Literature in 1995.

First impressions

When you first read Heaney's poems you may be conscious that they have a strong appeal to the senses. You may also notice that they are often related to events in his childhood and that these events can include violence and death, as well as humour at times. You will also find many references to the natural world and to working on the land, alongside a sense of the historical past and its parallels in modern times. If you listen to the poems you will hear their rhythmic flow and the writer's use of sound patterns.

ACTIVITY I

Work with a partner and read the poems through. Then complete the grid below, putting each poem under one or more headings.

Childhood	Land & nature	History & heritage	Violence/death
'An Advancement of Learning'	'An Advancement of Learning'		
'Ancestral Photograph'	'Ancestral Photograph'	'Ancestral Photograph'	

Discuss what your grid shows about the subjects and themes of the poems.

ACTIVITY 2

Work with a partner and read the poem 'Servant Boy'. Then do the following:

- select any words or phrases that give you clues to its meaning
- discuss any possible links between past and present you can find
- read a brief account of Irish history – you could search for one online
- read the poem again and discuss its meaning in this light.

Stretch your skills

Work with a partner and look at 'Blackberry-Picking', 'Digging' or 'Mid-Term Break'. Find a reading of one of these on YouTube and annotate the poem as you listen with notes on:

- the rhythm of the poem
- sound patterns you notice
- senses the poem appeals to
- images that are created.

Make a wall display of your poem by copying, enlarging and pasting it onto sugar paper. Include your annotations in boxes, using a different colour for each aspect. Colour code the quotations that match them by underlining or highlighting them.

Imagery

Seamus Heaney uses images that linger in the mind, such as 'Ears plastered down on his knobbed skull' (page 167) or 'big dark blobs burned/ Like a plate of eyes' (page 171). His images are exact, and he uses them to create feelings and atmospheres that make the reader part of the poems. Whether it is the child feeling 'the warm thick slobber/ Of frogspawn' (page 172) or the man looking at the body from the bog and imagining 'her shaved head/ like a stubble of black corn' (page 176), his images appeal vividly to the senses.

ACTIVITY 3

Work with a partner and copy the poem 'Death of a Naturalist'.

- Highlight all the words and phrases that describe sights.
- In a different colour, highlight all the words and phrases that describe sounds.
- In a different colour, highlight all the words and phrases that describe smells.

How and why do the descriptions in stanza 1 differ from those in stanza 2?

ACTIVITY 4

Work with a partner and look at the poem 'Ancestral Photograph'. Find an image that describes the following:

- the man in the photograph
- the space where it hung
- his great uncle at the fair.

Discuss Heaney's use of the following:

- 'Bullies the heavy mouth'
- 'Heckled and herded'
- 'penned in the frame'
- the final two lines.

Stretch your skills

Work with a partner to design a PowerPoint presentation for the imagery in 'Wheels within Wheels'. You could use the demonstration film of this poem on YouTube as part of it. Each slide should have an image from the poem with a quotation and a picture. You could include a narration of the poem and/or some suitable music as background.

Paste a copy of the poem onto a sheet of paper. Find all the words and phrases that refer to circular objects or movements. Highlight them and stick a picture of the objects next to them.

Language

Heaney's language can be very dense, and may require several readings to understand. It can also be really simple, as when he writes in the voice of a child about the tadpoles in 'Death of a Naturalist'. The references he includes to Irish history and culture can seem obscure unless you are familiar with them, but he also uses ideas and allusions that everyone will know. He has a habit of using hyphenated adjectives which make the words seem fresh. His metaphors are often extended to a stanza or a whole poem, as in 'Scaffolding', or the sedge-warbler in 'Serenades'.

ACTIVITY 5

Work with a partner and look at the poem 'Digging'. Find the following:

- three phrases that show his father's expertise with a spade
- three phrases that show his grandfather's skill at turf cutting
- three phrases that appeal to the senses
- two comparisons for the writer's pen.

Write two or three paragraphs about Heaney's use of language here.

ACTIVITY 6

Work with a partner and copy the poem 'Blackberry-Picking'. Highlight the comparisons – metaphors and similes – that Heaney uses in the poem.

List all the words and phrases that describe the senses. Divide the list into attractive and unattractive references.

Discuss your findings, then write a paragraph on Heaney's use of contrast between the two stanzas.

Structure

The poems here are varied, from 'Blackberry-Picking' and 'Death of a Naturalist', which both have two contrasting stanzas, through the formal four-line stanza structures of poems such as 'Punishment', 'Follower' and 'Serenades', to the uneven stanzas of 'Digging'. Heaney uses full rhymes, as well as half-rhymes and sound patterns, to create links and continuity. He also employs enjambment, often across stanzas, to connect ideas and make the verse flow, and caesura to emphasize a break. He uses these structures to make connections between past and present, childhood and adulthood, and across the generations, as in 'Ancestral Photograph'.

Stretch your skills

Look at the poem 'Punishment'. Complete the grid to show how Heaney implies deeper meanings in his phrases.

Quotation	Surface meaning	Connotations
'the frail rigging/ of her ribs'	The ribs are a framework	Rigging is used on ships, so she is seen as a sunken ship
'she was a barked sapling'		
'her blindfold a soiled bandage'		
'her noose a ring/ to store/ the memories of love'		
'the stones of silence'		
'your betraying sisters,/ cauled in tar'		
'the exact/ and tribal, intimate revenge'		

Write a paragraph about the language Heaney uses to connect past and present.

ACTIVITY 7

Look at the poem 'A Constable Calls'. Imagine that you are the child narrator and write the entry in your diary that covers the policeman's visit. Try to include your thoughts and feelings as they are described in the poem. What are you afraid of? What are the 'Small guilts' you assume? What do you think 'the black hole in the barracks' might be?

ACTIVITY 8

Work with a partner and look at the poem 'Scaffolding'. Answer the following questions.

- What is being described in the first two stanzas?
- What does the poem move on to in the third stanza?
- How is the metaphor revealed in the final two stanzas?
- How does the structure of the poem resemble the content?

Write a paragraph about Heaney's structure in this poem.

Stretch your skills

Work with a partner and look at the poem 'The Summer of Lost Rachel'. Copy and complete the boxes below with a brief overview of the subjects.

First three stanzas	Fourth stanza	Stanzas 5–7	Last two stanzas

Discuss why you think Heaney has used this structure. What does it add to the effect of the poem?

Look at the poet's use of rhyme and half-rhyme and discuss what it adds to the poem.

Heaney has used repetition as a structural device here. Identify where it is used and discuss how it adds to the meaning.

Personal response

There are a number of possible responses to Heaney's poems, ranging from humour to revulsion. He writes about human life as he has observed it as a child and as an adult looking back on his childhood. He remembers the joys and fears and anguish of growing up on a farm. He is very conscious of how human lives are tied to and moulded by the past, and by our families. The poems in the Anthology encompass death and violence, but also freedom and love. They are full of images of nature at its best and worst.

ACTIVITY 9

Work with a partner and look at the poem 'The Early Purges'. Discuss what Heaney is saying about town and country.

Write a leaflet, aimed at the public, based on the events in the poem. You should argue either for 'prevention of cruelty' or for 'keeping pests down'. Illustrate it with suitable pictures and quotations from the text.

ACTIVITY 10

Work with a partner and look at the poem 'Follower'. Imagine you are the narrator and you have been asked to take part in a new radio programme called 'Country memories'. Write the two-minute talk you would give on the radio, using the poem, with your own additions based on it, and including quotations where appropriate.

Stretch your skills

Choose one of Heaney's poems that you think should feature in a documentary about the author. Imagine you have been asked to direct this section of the documentary, and do the following:

- write a brief introduction to your poem – and a brief end piece after it
- make a storyboard including stills of the video recording you would include
- either find a reading of the poem, or make one yourself
- write a soundtrack to accompany the video, including any special effects and appropriate music you would include
- put your section of the documentary together on the computer.

HEANEY: SAMPLE TASKS

Sample task I (foundation level)

feelings, attitudes and images

interesting, important or memorable

In 'Mid-Term Break', **what** do you find **striking** about Heaney's **memories** of **his brother's death**?

the things he remembers and describes; the behaviour of adults

what it meant to him as a child

You should consider:

- the way he views events in the poem
- the way he describes other people's behaviour
- the words and phrases he uses.

Make a list of things to include in your answer, like the one below. You can tick them off as you write your answer.

Child's view of events

Underline appropriate quotations on the poem printed on the examination paper and number them to go with your notes.

1. He waits for a lift in the sick bay – word 'knelling' refers to funeral bell
2. His father is crying – unusual – why is this different?
3. Baby doesn't realize what's happened – inappropriate behaviour?
4. Embarrassed by adults – unusual respect; normally other way round
5. They whisper about him – tells the reader too
6. Mother seems angry – perhaps can't accept what has happened?
7. Sees little brother in coffin like a cot – emphasizes his youth

Some details that help to make it striking:

- 'it was a hard blow' – reader wants to find out what
- 'sorry for my trouble' – an Irish euphemism – colloquial speech
- 'stanched and bandaged by the nurses' – they had done what they could
- flowers and candles in room – religious symbols – seem to make it easier for mourners
- 'a poppy bruise on his left temple' – poppies are symbols of blood and death and also sacrifice (in war) – maybe child is seen as sacrifice
- 'the bumper knocked him clear' – tells reader he was run over – we only find out near the end
- 'a foot for every year' – we learn his age in last line – makes the poem sadder

SECTION 3

Sample task 2 (foundation level)

make it seem real and involve the reader

the good things and bad things about nature

How does Heaney **bring to life** some of the **joys and fears of nature** in **childhood** in **EITHER** 'Death of a Naturalist' **OR** 'Blackberry-Picking?

using feelings, situation and language

the way children see things as opposed to adults

Remember to refer closely to the words and phrases Heaney uses in your chosen poem.

Student response – Sample task I (foundation level)

In 'Mid-Term Break', Heaney is waiting in the school sick room. He can hear the class bell ringing and it reminds him why he is there because he uses the word 'knelling' which is a death bell. When he gets home he sees his father crying, which surprises him. I know this because it says 'He had always taken funerals in his stride'. The neighbours are there and some of them whisper about him, saying he is the eldest, which tells the reader this information as well.

He behaves as most children would when the old men stand up for him and says 'I was embarrassed' which most children would be as usually they have to stand up for adults. His mother takes his hand, which shows her affection and sympathy but she is also described as making 'angry tearless sighs'. This might mean she can't accept what has happened, but when we find out it is a road accident it makes me think she could be angry at the driver, knocking down a child.

The ambulance doesn't arrive until late, so Heaney doesn't see his little brother's body until the next day. When he goes into the bedroom he thinks the child is lying in the coffin just like he did in his cot. This is a very sad image because he must have been

shows understanding of language use

shows some understanding of how author uses structure

comments on writer's use of voice and viewpoint

appropriate personal response to an image which is explained quite well

well-chosen embedded quotation which is explained but not fully evaluated

good attempt to explain connotations of quotation but does not use technical term

very young if he was still in a cot. He notices 'a poppy bruise on his left temple'. I think Heaney is saying that the child was like a sacrifice because poppies are a symbol of blood and sacrifice in the two world wars.

At the end of the poem we find out the child was four because it says 'A four foot box, a foot for every year.' I think this is a sad way to end because the boy was only little and his coffin was little too, so it makes you think what a waste of a life.

Heaney uses good details like the baby laughing because it doesn't understand what happened, and flowers and candles in the bedroom like in church.

perceptive comment on use of symbols, and uses technical term correctly

good attempt to explain meaning and structure, although terminology not used

final comment on language use shows understanding of Heaney's imagery, but no real evaluation

EXAMINER'S COMMENTS OCR

- In their answer, this student engages well with the poem, offering personal responses to the poem and to the poet's language choices.
- Little knowledge of technical terms is shown, and analysis is minimal.

SECTION 3

Sample task 3 (higher level)

things a child fears and how they overcome this

How does Heaney convey the **fears and victories of childhood** in 'An Advancement of Learning'?

by using situation, feelings and language

Remember to refer closely to the language Heaney uses.

One way of planning your answer is to quickly list the points you want to include. You can number them and then use the poem printed on the paper to underline appropriate quotations and number them to correspond with your points.

1. Poem about a childhood fear – in this case of rats – how it's overcome – relate to title

2. How Heaney sets scene in first two stanzas: 'embankment path', 'river nosed past', 'transfer of gables and sky', 'dirty-keeled swans'

3. Tension of rat's appearance – 'Something slobbered' – unpleasant connotations

4. Situation as boy feels surrounded – 'throat sickened'

5. His feelings – 'in cold sweat' conveys horror of creatures

6. Language use – unusual (made-up?) verbs describing rats – 'slobbered', 'Slimed', 'nimbling', 'clockworked'; use of military terms – 'Bridgehead', 'trained on me', 'Retreated'

7. Boy's reaction to rat as he stares at it – 'deliberate, thrilled care'; how feelings change as he observes it closely

8. How final two stanzas tell of victory – 'Retreated up a pipe for sewage'

9. End of poem with symbolic bridge-crossing – going from childhood (irrational reactions) to adult (rational thoughts)

10. Use of voice and viewpoint – 'I' means reader is intimate with thoughts and feelings – therefore involved

11. Use of sound patterning (alliteration, assonance, consonance, onomatopoeia)

12. Bathos (at end) – 'This terror, cold, wet-furred, small-clawed'

13. Use of enjambment (linking across stanzas) and caesura (stops to create emphasis), rhyme scheme (usually lines 2 and 4, or 1 and 3)

Sample task 4 (higher level)

using situation, feelings and language

bring to life through images and details

How does Heaney **vividly portray** the **activities of a rural childhood** in **EITHER** 'Follower' **OR** 'Wheels within Wheels'?

Remember to refer closely to the language Heaney uses in your chosen poem.

things done by children in the country, rather than in town

Student response – Sample task 3 (higher level)

well-phrased brief overview; understands use of viewpoint

The title of the poem, 'An Advancement of Learning', refers to the way the narrator overcame a childhood fear of rats. The reader is involved by the use of the first-person viewpoint.

The first two stanzas of the poem describe 'the embankment path' and the river like an animal that 'nosed past,/ Pliable, oil-skinned'. This is a foretaste of the rodents he will face. The river's reflections are captured in the image of 'a transfer of gable and sky'. This sense of grubbiness is reinforced by 'the dirty-keeled swans', whose undersides are more like boats, covered with the oily water.

perceptive comment on structure and meaning

thoughtful points on imagery with evaluations

When a rat appears it is described by words such as 'slobbered', 'Smudging' and 'Slimed' which are both alliterative and unpleasant, like the rat itself. This image conveys Heaney's distaste and this is emphasized by the phrase 'My throat sickened'. This reaction of feeling sick shows his real fear of the rodent especially when combined with 'in cold sweat', which afflicts him as he turns to go back but sees he is trapped, as another rat 'was nimbling/ Up the far bank'. This is an unusual verb which implies speed and the use of claws. Having established the boy's real fear, Heaney marks the turning point with a caesura before 'Incredibly', a word the reader can see as appropriate.

well-selected quotations to support language use comments

use of technical term to show understanding of Heaney's techniques and language

fluent use of embedded quotations

Student response – Sample task 3 (higher level) continued

shows a sound appreciation of Heaney's choice of terms and verbs

use of technical term in right context

The child's sudden resolution is told in the military term 'established a... Bridgehead', which means that he held his ground and stared the rodent out. He sees the rat as it really is and Heaney describes its movements as 'clockworked aimlessly', which compares it with a harmless clockwork toy. The details of 'knobbed skull' and 'raindrop eye' reinforce the rat's ugly but unthreatening appearance, although the phrase 'trained on me' implies a sniper. As the boy forgets his previous panic about rats, Heaney uses bathos to show 'This terror' is really 'cold, wet-furred, small-clawed'. It 'Retreated', a word that suggests defeat, and the boy knows he has conquered his fear. The final phrase 'crossed the bridge' is a metaphor for his crossing from fear to victory over it.

shows ability to decipher implied meanings and to explain and evaluate them

good comprehension of metaphor, but could have suggested other possible meanings

EXAMINER'S COMMENTS OCR
RECOGNISING ACHIEVEMENT

- This is an elegant answer, closely focused on the question but demonstrating an excellent grasp of literary techniques and the effect of each on this poem.
- This is a very strong Higher Tier response.

Benjamin Zephaniah was brought up in Handsworth, Birmingham and moved to London in the 1980s. He became famous as a dub poet, performing his work all over the world. He has received a number of honorary degrees from various universities, despite leaving school at 15. He has turned down honours, including the offer of an OBE. He has also written several novels for teenagers. He now lives in Spalding, Lincolnshire and in Beijing, China.

First impressions

One of the first things you will notice about Zephaniah's poetry is how political it is. His aim is to give a voice to those minorities in society who are not usually heard, or are suppressed altogether. This is true whether he is writing about Britain, South Africa before Nelson Mandela was released from prison, or countries in Asia. His anger at oppression and his passion for justice shine through his poetry, from 'Biko the Greatness' to 'What Stephen Lawrence Has Taught Us'. Even if you don't know the details of the cases he refers to in some poems, the principles for which he stands are clear.

ACTIVITY I

Work with a partner and choose six of Zephaniah's poems. Take turns to read the poems aloud. Listeners should jot down whatever comes into their heads as they listen. Compare notes about your thoughts and see whether a pattern emerges. Organize your jottings into a concept map or a written paragraph.

ACTIVITY 2

Look at the quotations below and group them into two lists, headed 'Personal' and 'Political'.

'Your luv may lie an yet be true'

'Wickedness tried to kill greatness'

'How our souls were sold'

'Ana Pereira is chewing bloodstained oats'

'Jimmy's getting old now'

'Dere's more to luv dan luv'

Compare your list with a partner and discuss what this suggests about the poems.

Imagery

Zephaniah uses imagery sparingly in his poems, but he can bring an idea or scene vividly to life in a phrase such as 'She prayed uncontrollably' (page 188), which depicts someone who is frantic, or 'dis dumb, unfeeling cell' (page 190), where he makes the room symbolize his captors. His images are most notable when showing people who are desperate or oppressed, but they can be more light-hearted, as when he summarizes adolescence as 'The snoring and the shaving/ A place to squeeze your spots' (page 192). Mainly his images are political, such as 'The only photo of dis child/ Was her corpse' (page 198).

Stretch your skills

Work with a partner and look at the poem 'Three Black Males'. Answer the following questions:

- Which three injustices are mentioned in stanza 1?
- In stanza 1, when are black people 'in white nations'?
- Write down two points made about 'the system' in stanza 2.
- What is 'the system'?
- In stanza 3, how are the three named men compared with the Home Office?
- What is the poet saying about democracy in the final stanza?

Use a search engine to look for the named men and read about their case on the Internet. What does your research add to your understanding of the poem?

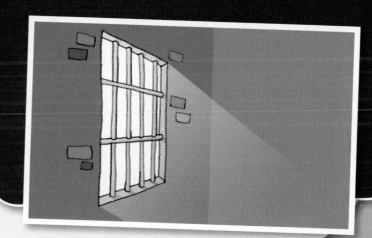

ACTIVITY 3

Work with a partner and look at the poem 'Chant of a Homesick Nigga'. Create a Powerpoint presentation which uses this poem to show police attitudes towards black men. You will need the following:

- pictures – preferably showing images from the poem
- captions – using quotations from the poem
- music and/or sound effects that enhance it.

Compare presentations with others in the class.

ACTIVITY 4

Work with a partner and look at the poem 'What Stephen Lawrence Has Taught Us'. Highlight the following phrases:

'sick Mussolinis'

'angels of death'

'Chips on their shoulders'

'injustice on their backs'

'the trading standards'

'emptying our pockets on the pavements'

'friends in high places'

'Teletubby land'

Discuss what the phrases suggest and why Zephaniah has used them.

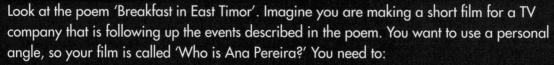

Stretch your skills

Look at the poem 'Breakfast in East Timor'. Imagine you are making a short film for a TV company that is following up the events described in the poem. You want to use a personal angle, so your film is called 'Who is Ana Pereira?' You need to:

- find photographs to use as background images
- write a narrative to accompany the pictures, using words and phrases from the poem
- write the script of an interview with Ana Pereira, using quotations and ideas from the poem
- find appropriate music to use at intervals.

Language

Zephaniah uses a mixture of black English, traditional sayings, and colloquial and formal language to convey his ideas. One of his main themes is the way in which language can be used to cover up what is really happening, and to promote injustice and oppression. He uses biblical and literary allusions as well as phrases from news reports to make readers aware of the historical nature of repression and struggle. Zephaniah also makes use of dialogue to create a feeling of immediacy, and uses the first-person viewpoint to involve the reader.

ACTIVITY 5

Discuss with a partner what Zephaniah is saying about black artists in the poem 'Bought and Sold'. Who do you think the poem is addressed to?

Write an open letter to a national newspaper addressing black British poets and performers. Write what the poet is saying in your own words, but include quotations from the poem where appropriate.

ACTIVITY 6

Look at the poem 'What If', and find a copy of the poem 'If' by Rudyard Kipling. Highlight all the words and phrases in Zephaniah's version that come from Kipling's poem. Write a blog for an online poetry website about how the poet has used this famous poem to mean something both similar and different by changing its language.

Stretch your skills

The poem 'Having a Word' is all about language use. Make a list of the words that Zephaniah questions in the poem, such as 'equality', 'democracy' and 'security'. Complete a grid like the one below.

Word from poem	Normal, accepted meaning	Zephaniah's meaning in poem
'equality'	Everyone treated the same in a good way	Everyone oppressed in the same way
'together'	Everyone in accord with one another	Everyone put together but not in agreement or united

Prepare a handout for the class with the two different meanings you have identified, shown as colour-coded annotations to the poem.

Structure

Because he is a performance poet, Zephaniah's poems tend to be very rhythmic, with a strong rhyme scheme linking ideas. They usually have a central argument which is carried through different aspects and varying emphases. Many of them are 'protest poems' which make their point through repetition, as in 'Biko the Greatness' and 'Chant of a Homesick Nigga'. Others are more personal and use repetitive humour, such as 'Jimmy Grows Old' and 'Press Ups an Sit Ups'. Zephaniah also uses the form of a conversation, as in 'Reminders' and 'Room for Rent', to show different viewpoints.

ACTIVITY 7

The poem 'Reminders' shows the same scene through opposing viewpoints. Work with a partner and imagine you are writing a scene in a play where the two characters meet after many years. Write a brief dialogue for the roles of the 'old soldier' and the 'old pacifist'. Use your own words, based closely on the poem.

ACTIVITY 8

Work with a partner to prepare the poem 'Deep in Luv' for performance. Notice the way in which Zephaniah uses repetition as an underlying structure for the poem. Decide how you can best bring this out in performance – perhaps through speaking alternate lines, taking a sentence each or perhaps a stanza each. Try different methods and decide which works best.

Stretch your skills

Look at the poem 'Jimmy Grows Old'. With a partner, do the following:

- highlight the phrases that tell us what Jimmy used to be like
- highlight the phrases that say what he is like now
- divide two sheets of paper into squares to resemble comic book pages
- draw cartoon pictures of what Jimmy was like, with captions taken from the poem, on the first page
- draw cartoon pictures of what Jimmy is like now, with captions taken from the poem, on the second page.

Write a paragraph about Zephaniah's use of structure to help the reader understand the poem.

Personal response

Your response to Zephaniah's poems may be emotional or rational. His pleas for justice for oppressed people are both full of feeling and thoughtful. He writes of policemen literally getting away with murder, of authorities who don't investigate cases fully, and of the hypocrisy of a society that claims to be democratic but gives people no voice beyond the ballot box. He questions 'institutional racism' not only in Britain but in societies across the world. However, he can also write humorously about the ways we try to show love or keep fit.

ACTIVITY 9

In the poem 'Adultery', Zephaniah questions whether we really want honesty in our relationships. Organize a five-minute debate where two speakers argue that we need total honesty in society, and two speakers argue that honesty can be damaging at times. There should be a chairperson to monitor the speakers, and they should use quotations from the poem to support their viewpoints.

ACTIVITY 10

Design a leaflet based on the poem 'Press Ups an Sit Ups' to advise people how to keep fit. To make it as appealing as possible, you should include:

- pictures of the activities mentioned
- quotations from the poem linked to the pictures
- advice from the poet – perhaps in the form of an interview
- a section on FAQs (frequently asked questions).

Stretch your skills

Work with a partner, looking at the poem 'Room for Rent'. Write a short play to be broadcast on the radio in which a black man with dreadlocks tries to rent a room. You should include each of his three attempts, and the excuses he is given. You can use the man as a narrator, speaking his thoughts, and include your own dialogue for his conversations with the landlords. Use quotations from the poem wherever possible.

You could record your play when it is finished, using members of the class to play the roles, and then broadcast it.

ZEPHANIAH: SAMPLE TASKS

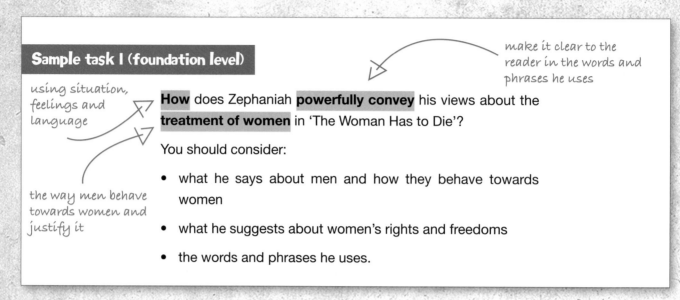

Sample task I (foundation level)

using situation, feelings and language

the way men behave towards women and justify it

How does Zephaniah **powerfully convey** his views about the **treatment of women** in 'The Woman Has to Die'?

make it clear to the reader in the words and phrases he uses

You should consider:

- what he says about men and how they behave towards women
- what he suggests about women's rights and freedoms
- the words and phrases he uses.

One way of planning an answer is a concept map like the one below, which starts with the poem and then branches out.

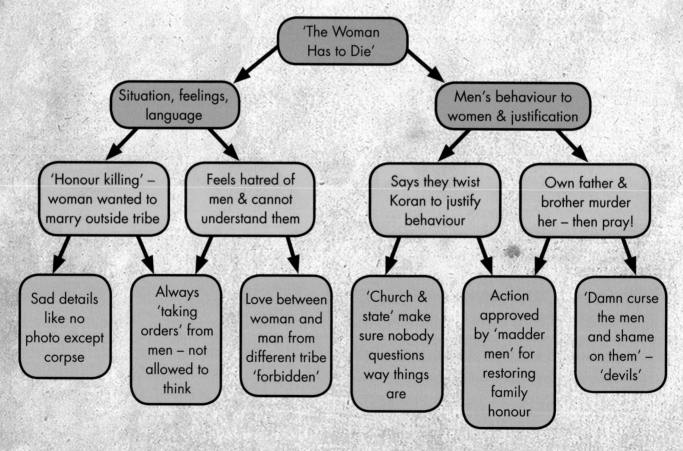

You could underline the quotations you want to use on the poem printed in the examination paper, and use numbers to link them to the appropriate boxes.

Write a brief outline plan to give your structure:

- introduction giving a short overview of the poem and the main theme
- the way Zephaniah tells us about the woman's growing up
- the words and phrases that Zephaniah uses to tell us the situation that led to her death
- the way in which the poet describes the woman's fate
- Zephaniah's comments on the murder and the people who committed it
- conclusion giving brief comments on structure and how it helps understanding of the poem.

Sample task 2 (foundation level)

using situation, feelings, language and structure

how he makes the events and situations amusing

How does Zephaniah **use humour** to convey the **joys and frustrations of human life** in **EITHER** 'Deep in Luv' **OR** 'Press Ups an Sit Ups'?

Remember to refer closely to the words and phrases Zephaniah uses in your chosen poem.

the good things that happen and the annoying or irritating ones

---

Student response – Sample task I (foundation level)

sound overview of what poem is about

In this poem Zephaniah is saying that women in some Islamic countries have no rights and no freedom. They have to do what men tell them or they will be killed, like the woman in the poem who fell in love with a man from another tribe.

understanding of cultural background used in poem, although limited

good use of evidence to support points and some attempt at evaluation

She was not even allowed to think what she liked. I know this because it says 'Her free thinking was deemed as sin' which means it was against their religion. Zephaniah also writes that it was a 'twisted faith' so it wasn't true to the Koran.

thoughtful point about the idea that no difference in religion separated them – could have expanded it

perceptive point that men have support of church and state

In the second stanza it says that she was in love with a man from another place in the same country and he loved her. Even though he was a Muslim too their love was 'forbidden' because he wasn't chosen by her parents. He says that both the church and the state will support the father whatever he does.

Then Zephaniah says that the woman's father got her own brother to shoot her dead and then 'they both knelt down to pray'. I think it is shocking to think that these men could pray to God after doing such a horrible crime. It is given the name of 'honour killing' but Zephaniah says it is only 'madder men' than them who will 'sing their praises'.

well-presented personal response to poem, linked to social ideas

fluent use of embedded quotations

Benjamin Zephaniah uses very strong language to say what he thinks about this murder. He writes 'Damn curse the men and shame on them' and he also says 'These devils are not God's men' which tells us he does not believe their religion would really tell them to murder an innocent woman.

comment on Zephaniah's language, which needs expanding

The last thing that Zephaniah writes about is the fact that there is no photo of the woman, which is repeating what he said at the beginning of the poem. 'There is no photo of her smile', instead all there is is a picture of the corpse in the newspaper. I think this makes it even sadder because this is the only way she will remembered – as a dead body, instead of a living smiling woman.

lack of technical terms and detailed evaluation

fair point about use of emotive detail and the poet's intentions

EXAMINER'S COMMENTS OCR

- This Foundation Tier answer shows some understanding of the poem and some interesting personal responses from the student.
- The student has not focused enough on the detail of the language used in the poem, or demonstrated understanding of technical terms.

Sample task 3 (higher level)

using situation, feelings, language and structure

how he makes the reader aware of how strong they are

In what ways does Zephaniah **powerfully convey** his feelings **about freedom and justice** in 'Biko the Greatness'?

Remember to refer closely to the language he uses.

being free within the state and not oppressed

One way of planning your answer is to make a list of points to include like the one below.

Situation
- South Africa under apartheid laws

- the murder of Steve Biko, civil rights activist, in police custody

- how his life and death inspired others to keep fighting until the regime was overthrown – doctors, nurses, educators, children

Feelings
- anger against the 'white tyrants' who oppressed the black majority

- celebration of Steve Biko and his inspiration for others

- happiness and relief that black people won freedom not just in SA but elsewhere

Structure
- lack of regular rhyme scheme – reliance on rhythm of words

- use of repetition – need to 'hear' poem in your head as performance

- moves outwards from individuals to society, country and world

- form of eulogy to Biko

Language use
- personification – 'wickedness', 'greatness', 'truth' – emphasize their importance as opposing forces

- reversals – 'downpressed', 'overstand' – give fresh perspective on meanings

- religious allusion – 'valley of the shadow of death' – often used at funerals, Psalm 23: 'I will fear no evil'

- metaphor – 'wind of change', 'the God complex' – Harold Macmillan in speech to SA government: 'The wind of change is blowing through this continent. Whether we like it or not, this growth of national consciousness is a political fact.'

- contrast – wickedness v. greatness; oppression v. freedom; white v. black

- memorable phrase – 'nobody dies until they're forgotten' – to show Biko is not forgotten, therefore not dead in some way

Student response – Sample task 3 (higher level)

In this poem Zephaniah shows his admiration of Steve Biko by associating him with the personification of greatness. He shows his abhorrence of the regime that killed him by personifying it as wickedness. He sets these two concepts in opposition throughout the poem, which tells of how Biko's death inspired the black majority to fight for freedom.

understands use of personification and uses technical term

well-expressed summary of poem

Zephaniah begins by asserting that the white South African government assumed that 'One could not hear the cries of another' in 'a corner of South Africa', which suggests they believed they could act with impunity since the victims' families were effectively silenced. He writes of them as 'No mothers and fathers/ No sisters and brothers' but as he later makes clear, the whole of black South Africa stood together as a family against the 'white tyrants', inspired by Biko's example.

fluent and accurate use of embedded quotations

very perceptive and thorough evaluation of poet's meaning and intentions

Zephaniah uses reversals in 'downpressed' and 'overstand' to make the reader notice his ideas about oppression and understanding. To press down seems even harsher than to oppress, while 'overstand' has connotations of an arrogance that doesn't want to understand. His reference to 'the God complex' reinforces this view.

detailed and intelligent comments about language use

uses technical terms with confidence

SECTION 3

relates details
to question
throughout

Zephaniah's feelings are of celebration for the life of Steve Biko and what he achieved. He is seen as 'The greatness that inspired doctors and nurses' to fight for freedom and 'educators to become liberators'. The professional class are seen as being in the forefront of the freedom movement because of their place in society. He describes black South Africans as 'in the valley of the shadow of death', a reference to the 23rd Psalm, which also talks of fearing no evil because God is with them, a phrase that Zephaniah uses to place 'Biko the Greatness' in the role of God. He follows this by quoting from Harold Macmillan's speech to the South African government about 'the wind of change' blowing through the continent, here associated with 'Greatness was its trustee, guided by truth'.

He concludes his poem with joyful feelings because 'wickedness is dead'. The legacy of Biko lives on through artistic performances and 'nobody dies until they're forgotten', meaning his memory lives on.

sound
research and
knowledge
of original
sources
and how
Zephaniah
uses them

good
conclusion
but a little
hasty – could
have been
expanded

EXAMINER'S COMMENTS OCR

- This is a strong response, showing a sensitive understanding of the context of the poem and of the poet's writing.
- Effective analysis of the poet's language is included, supported by apt quotations from the poem.
- Although the conclusion could be improved, this is a very strong answer within the Higher Tier.

Great Clarendon Street, Oxford OX2 6DP

Oxford University Press is a department of the University of Oxford.
It furthers the University's objective of excellence in research,
scholarship, and education by publishing worldwide in

Oxford   New York

Auckland   Cape Town   Dar es Salaam   Hong Kong   Karachi
Kuala Lumpur   Madrid   Melbourne   Mexico City   Nairobi
New Delhi   Shanghai   Taipei   Toronto

With offices in

Argentina   Austria   Brazil   Chile   Czech Republic   France   Greece
Guatemala   Hungary   Italy   Japan   Poland   Portugal   Singapore
South Korea   Switzerland   Thailand   Turkey   Ukraine   Vietnam

Oxford is a registered trade mark of Oxford University Press
in the UK and in certain other countries

© Oxford University Press 2011

Authors: Annie Fox, Angela Topping, Carmel Waldron
The moral rights of the authors have been asserted.

Database right Oxford University Press (maker)

First published 2011

Third party website addresses referred to in this publication are
provided by Oxford University Press in good faith and for
information only and Oxford University Press disclaims any
responsibility for the material contained therein

British Library Cataloguing in Publication Data

Data available

ISBN 978-0-19-912858-7

10 9 8 7 6 5 4 3 2 1

Printed in Spain by Cayfosa-Impressia Ibérica

Paper used in the production of this book is a natural, recyclable product
made from wood grown in sustainable forests. The manufacturing process
conforms to the environmental regulations of the country of origin.

Acknowledgements

The publisher and authors would like to thank the following for their
permission to reproduce photographs and other copyright material:

p6: Andy Farrer/Shutterstock; **p7l:** photobar/Shutterstock; **p7r:** Marish/
Shutterstock; **p8:** Isabella Pfenninger/Shutterstock; **p9l:** Berents/
Shutterstock; **p9r:** Scorpp/Shutterstock; **p10:** SSPL/NMeM/Daily Herald
Archive/Getty Images; **p11:** OUP; **p12:** Angelo Hornak/Alamy; **p15tr:**
Zorani/istockphoto; **p15bl:** Olga Ryabtsova/istockphoto; **p18:** Hulton
Archive/Stringer/Getty Images; **p19:** T.M.O.Birds/Alamy; **p20t:** Mike Brake/
Shutterstock; **p20b:** Marilyn Barbone/Shutterstock; **p21:** Hannamariah/
Shutterstock; **p28:** Mariait/Shutterstock; **p26tl:** Archive Photos/Stringer/
Hulton Archive/Getty Images; **p26br:** Mary Evans Picture Library/Alamy;
p28: Tim Gainey/Alamy; **p30tl:** Mary Evans Picture Library/Alamy; **p30tr:**
Mary Evans Picture Library/Alamy; **p30b:** Mary Evans Picture Library/Alamy;
p34: Lebrecht Music & Arts Photo Library/Photolibrary; **p35:** Mary Evans
Picture Library/Alamy; **p36:** Classic Image/Alamy; **p37:** Courtesy of Dorset
County Museum: Thomas Hardy Memorial Collection; **p42:** Lebrecht Music
& Arts Photo Library; **p43:** The Print Collector/Alamy; **p44:** Scott Rothstein/
Shutterstock; **p45:** With kind permission of the Trustees of the Owen
Estate; **p46:** Thieury/Shutterstock; **p50:** Hulton Archive/Stringer/Getty
Images; **p51:** AlaskaStock/Corbis; **p53:** Andreja Donko/Shutterstock; **p58:**
Time & Life Pictures/Getty Images; **p59:** Dwight Nadig/istockphoto; **p61:**
Samantha Scott/Alamy; **p62:** Sklep Spozywczy/Shutterstock; **p68:** David
Levenson/Getty Images; **p69:** alxpin/istockphoto; **p70tr:** flab/Alamy; **p70bl:**
Clynt Garnham Publishing/Alamy; **p80:** Keith Morris/Alamy; **p81:** AVTG/
istockphoto; **p82:** Todd Keith/istockphoto; **p85:** Koray ISIK/iStockphoto ;
p92t: Rex Features; **p92b:** blickwinkel/Alamy; **p94:** travelib europe/Alamy;
p96: OtnaYdur /Shutterstock; **p104t:** Christopher Furlong/Getty Images;
p104b: Alexander Raths/Shutterstock; **p105:** LIGHTWORK/Shutterstock;
p106: Perry Correll/Shutterstock; **p108:** Yellowj/Shutterstock; **p116:** David
Levenson/Contributor/Getty Images; **p117:** Birute Vijeikiene/Shutterstock;
p118: Ivonne Wierink/Shutterstock; **p119:** Joe Belanger/Shutterstock;
p128: Susannah Ireland/Rex Features; **p130:** The Photolibrary Wales/Alamy;
p130: Monkey Business Images/Shutterstock; **p144:** Susannah Ireland/Rex
Features.

Illustrations by Jorge/Beehive.